REFLECTIONS OF ELEGANCE

Cartier Jewels from the Lindemann Collection

REFLECTIONS OF ELEGANCE

Cartier Jewels from the Lindemann Collection

Essay Contributors

The Honorable Harry St. C. Fane
Hans Nadelhoffer
Eric Nussbaum
John W. Keefe
Darrell Lee Brown

New Orleans Museum of Art
New Orleans, Louisiana
1988

This exhibition and catalogue were made possible in part
by a generous gift from George and Frayda Lindemann.

Exhibition Schedule:

New Orleans Museum of Art, New Orleans, LA   November 13, 1988-February 12, 1989
Birmingham Museum of Art, Birmingham, AL   April 14-May 30, 1989
The Walters Art Gallery, Baltimore, MD   August 27-October 15, 1989
San Diego Museum of Art, San Diego, CA   November 17-December 31, 1989

Copies of the catalogue are available from the New Orleans Museum of Art,
P.O. Box 19123, New Orleans, LA 70179.

ISBN 0-89494-029-5
ISBN 0-89494-030-9 (paper)

Photography by Michael Oldford, New York.
Design by Ed Biggs, Gretna, Louisiana.
Typography by Paragraphics, Inc., New Orleans.
Printing by Balding + Mansell International, Ltd., Wisbech, England.

Front cover photo "Mandarin Duck" Mystery clock, 1922
Topaz, jade, ruby, onyx, diamond, enamel, gold, and platinum
Ht. $10^1/_2''$ W. 6" D. 4"
(see catalogue number LXIV)

Inside front and back cover photos
Temple brooch, 1927
Diamond and platinum
Ht. $1^3/_8''$ W. $^{11}/_{16}''$ D. $^1/_4''$
(see catalogue number VII)

DEDICATION

We respectfully dedicate this catalogue to our good friend and advisor, Hans Nadelhoffer, whose untimely death sadly coincides with the first public exhibition of our collection. His influence can be found throughout these pages, and we can still hear him enthusiastically describing some new and wonderful Cartier discovery. All of those who shared his respect for these beautiful objects shall miss him.

Frayda and George Lindemann

EDITOR'S NOTES

Authors are listed on the title page in order of the appearance of their articles in the catalogue.

European spellings occur in accordance with their usage by the particular author.

Objects in the exhibition have been divided into three groups for purposes of their reproduction in the catalogue and are arranged as much as possible in chronological sequence within each group.

When exact dating is not possible, reference is made to similar datable objects.

Unless otherwise stated in text, all Roman numerals refer to color plates and all Arabic numerals refer to text pages.

All color illustrations are as close as possible to actual size.

All pearls are natural and are not cultivated.

In all cases, the materials used in the descriptions of the flowers refer only to the flowers themselves, and not to the materials of which the vitrines are fabricated.

Photographic credits: All photographs are by Michael Oldford, New York, unless otherwise noted.

TABLE OF CONTENTS

CURATORIAL ACKNOWLEDGEMENTS

Although previous museum tenures had provided the opportunity to work and become familiar with such celebrated names in the history of modern jewelry as Peter Carl Fabergé, René Lalique, Louis Comfort Tiffany, and Henri Vever, the Lindemann Collection offered the first occasion to know the creations of the great House of Cartier. Therefore, I am grateful for the exposure to these beautiful objects, and I am indebted to the Lindemanns for the hospitality extended to me as the collection was catalogued. It was a pleasure to work with such dedicated and impassioned collectors whose files alone would put many a museum to shame. I am particularly grateful to Frayda Lindemann for her supervision of the complex photography with Michael Oldford in New York. She then came to New Orleans and cheerfully reviewed each transparency, taking back with her those which we felt could be improved. It was she who also patiently permitted her schedule to be disrupted repeatedly as calls from New Orleans came in carrying with them myriad detailed questions about individual objects. Without fail, those questions were answered promptly; every curator should be so fortunate in his or her dealings with a collector.

George Lindemann has obviously gathered an extraordinary staff at Metro Mobile CTS. On behalf of the museum, I am particularly grateful to Tilda Schiehle, Administrative Assistant to the Chairman, who gracefully and efficiently coped with many details of the exhibition. It was she who carefully forwarded a host of questions, installation information and cataloguing problems to Mr. and Mrs. Lindemann whenever they were away from New York. Diane Ellmann, Assistant to the President at Metro Mobile, also assisted us with the many unseen details which inevitably appear as an exhibition of this scope evolves.

For much the same reason, a special expression of thanks is owed to the late Hans Nadelhoffer, author of this catalogue's primary essay and of the pioneering volume, *Cartier: Jewelers Extraordinary*. Mr. Nadelhoffer and his office graciously answered many of the questions which arose as the catalogue developed. Eric Nussbaum, director of Cartier *Haute Joallerie*, Geneva, Switzerland, and Curator

of the Museé Cartier there, also assisted with numerous historical details and provided answers to a host of questions. I am indebted to Monsieur Alain Cartier, Paris, for his helpful comments on the important "Mandarin Duck" Mystery clock and to Dr. Donald A. Wood, Curator of Oriental Art, the Birmingham Museum of Art, Birmingham, Alabama, for his explanation of the traditional Oriental iconographies as they related to the products of the House of Cartier. The museum's librarian, Carl Penny, generously offerred to proofread the catalogue text, as did Wanda O'Shello, editor of the museum's house publication *Arts Quarterly*. Their input was invaluable in perceiving problems which had eluded those of us who had written, read and reread the text. Nancy Kittay of Nancy Kittay Jewels, New Orleans, was unstintingly generous with her expertise and time as technical questions arose about gemstone cuts and settings.

A particular note of appreciation and thanks is owed to Darrell Lee Brown, Curatorial Assistant at the Museum, who was also being exposed to the fabulous creations of Cartier for the first time. He enthusiastically and persistently assisted with every phase of preparation of the catalogue notes. It was also he who entered the enormous amount of data involved with the catalogue in the museum's computer system. As his knowledge of the history of jewelry grew and his familiarity with the House of Cartier expanded, his insights and consultation became invaluable to this project.

To the Museum's registrar, Daniel E. Piersol and his assistant Paul Tarver, I am indebted for their painstaking assistance in packing these precious and fragile objects. Their safe arrival in New Orleans and arrangements for their ongoing travel were in large part due to their dedication to this complicated facet of the exhibition.

The successful exhibition catalogue always appears to have fallen into place effortlessly. Should this catalogue fall into that category, its production is due to the dedicated work of Ed Biggs, Gretna, Louisiana, who competently and patiently dealt with the inevitable debates regarding format, spacing, color and other technical matters. Mr. Biggs also formed an effective liaison with Balding +

Mansell International, Ltd. in Wisbech, Cambridgeshire, thus removing a great deal of cataloguing pressure from the curatorial offices.

Any exhibition of this magnitude requires the assistance of many staff members who are frequently unseen but without whose help the installation could not take place. Chief Preparator Thom Herrington and all of those who work under his supervision are to be thanked for their cooperation. A properly installed exhibition should appear to have almost arranged itself; however, this is generally not the case, particularly when working with small objects each one of which presents an independent sculptural problem. Without the advice of Mr. Herrington and the preparators, the exhibition could not have assumed its sleek and tailored appearance.

Finally, a sincere thank you to Director, E. John Bullard who patiently suffered the occasional bouts of frustration and even ill temper which accompany the preparation of a detailed catalogue. I can only hope that he and the board of trustees of the New Orleans Museum of Art regard the finished product as worth all of the time and effort. I certainly do.

John W. Keefe
Principal Curator of Decorative Arts
New Orleans Museum of Art

DIRECTOR'S STATEMENT

It is always a happy occasion when an art museum is afforded the opportunity to organize an exhibition of a collection of the importance and beauty of the Cartier jewels and *objets de vertu* assembled by Frayda and George Lindemann. A series of fortuitous coincidences, notably George Lindemann's longstanding friendship with Dr. Kurt A. Gitter, one of our Museum's most dedicated trustees, brought the Lindemann Collection to New Orleans and, ultimately, to the other American museums on the national tour. Dr. Gitter and his wife, Alice Rae Yelen, suggested to the Lindemanns that their collection was worthy of public exhibition and tour. A meeting was arranged in New Orleans at which I and our Curator of Decorative Arts, John W. Keefe, viewed some of the smaller objects in the collection and looked at transparencies of the others. The air that evening crackled with enthusiasm and excitement as we saw the genius of Cartier reflected in these superb pieces.

At their best, art museums should set standards of quality and attempt to formulate public taste. Therefore, it is a double pleasure for the New Orleans Museum of Art to premier the Lindemann Collection. For all too long a time, the production of the House of Cartier has been looked upon as extravagant costume accessory and expensive ephemera. That point of view began to change in the late 1970 s with such benchmark events as the H. Robert Greene sale of Art Deco objects at Christie's International in 1978. The awakening recognition of Cartier and its production was dramatically advanced by the 1981 publication of Hans Nadelhoffer's brilliant pioneering volume on the House of Cartier. Today, the firm is internationally recognized as a distinguished and innovative fabricator of some of the world's most important jeweled objects, a worthy standard bearer of the finest principles of design and craft inherited from the Renaissance. Cartier's pieces are today universally seen as part of the mainstream of European decorative arts history.

The jewels and *objets de vertu* seen in the exhibition and illustrated in the catalogue are a testimony to the taste, discrimination and determination of Frayda and George Lindemann, who have searched the world for the finest examples of Cartier's astonishing and varied productivity. The collection is all the more remarkable when one realizes that it has been assembled in the relatively short span of the past eight years. The New Orleans Museum of Art and the other American museums presenting this exhibition are profoundly grateful to the Lindemanns for their generosity in sharing their Cartier treasures with the American public for such an extended period of time.

E. John Bullard, Director
New Orleans Museum of Art

COLLECTORS' NOTES

Our collection of Cartier treasures actually began quite modestly, in fact, almost accidently. Throughout the 1960s and early '70s my husband George collected eighteenth and nineteenth-century watches and clocks, a rather specialized field of interest with its own curators and dealers. Cartier clocks, watches and objects, on the other hand, are considered the province of the jeweler and the jewelry departments of public auction houses; although loudly ticking antique clocks and watches filled our home, the wonderful world of Cartier still eluded our attention.

Around 1975, I began to notice the pretty, wearable Cartier brooches which would appear now and then in Sotheby's and Christie's jewelry sales; these attractive pieces of jewelry actually became the foundation of our collection. During a visit to Paris in the late 1970s, while strolling past the House of Cartier near the Place Vendôme, we noticed some marvelous jeweled clocks in vitrines. These extravagant timepieces were being used as decorations for the modern jewelry displays. A very courteous salesman indulged our interest and brought out two important clocks from the Cartier Museum collection, the famous "Carp" clock from the *animalia* series and one of the crystal "Portico" models. We were enchanted and talked for weeks after we returned home about acquiring some of these marvelous treasures.

It was Eric Nussbaum, director of the Cartier Museum, who gave us the opportunity to acquire our first important clock. When Eric showed us a picture of the "Mandarin Duck" Mystery clock (catalogue number LXIV) we were lukewarm about this first example of the twelve *animalia* clocks (1922). Fortunately, Eric insisted that we examine the clock in person. He carried it all the way from Paris to New York, whereupon we fell in love with its sweet expression and spectacular faceted topaz dial. It is appropriate that this early acquisition serve as an icon of our collection and we delight in seeing its picture again and again on bookcovers and posters.

An additional personal reward of our first major acquisition was the friendship it engendered with Eric Nussbaum. Eric has held our hand throughout the years, teaching, guiding, researching, sometimes enticing us, often infecting us with his own admiration for these beautiful objects. The assembling of our collection has been a saga of exciting discoveries and wonderful personal relationships, none more significant than our friendship with Eric Nussbaum.

Following that important first acquisition of the large clock, the years have been filled with learning, acquiring, selling, combing foreign cities for unexpected surprises and, of course, keeping in touch with special friends we have met through this mutual passion. One very special English friend, Harry St. C. Fane, has virtually scoured the world in search of precious Cartier objects, having luckily turned his avocation into a vocation. At the drop of a hat, Harry will fly from Geneva to Bombay, Buenos Aires or New York on the trail of a special piece. Many of our most favorite objects were found for us by Harry and from our very first encounter the Lindemanns and the Fanes have been aesthetic kindred spirits. It was Harry who found for us the very rare and early *(circa* 1915) Obelisk clock (catalogue number LV). Our son Adam, who collects French Empire furniture and decorations, especially likes the obelisk form so admired in the Napoleonic era. Planning for a special birthday, I asked Harry if he could possibly locate the rare clock I knew only from its depiction in the Greene Collection sale catalog of 1978. In a stroke of good luck and perfect timing, Harry relocated the piece, and we presented it to Adam on the correct day. To my knowledge, it is the only extant specimen of this model in pristine condition.

During the last five years, our collection has been displayed in a pair of lovely Georgian cabinets flanking the chimneypiece of our living room in New York. It is a great delight to our families and close friends who come to dinner, and my husband George, a typically proud and enthusiastic collector, takes pride in explaining and showing off each new acquisition to his captive audience. We have always considered these Cartier pieces to be a private reflection of our own taste and interest. It was Dr. Kurt Gitter, a dear friend since childhood, and his wife Alice Rae Yelen who suggested the idea that our collection might be of public interest in a museum setting. Alice, Special Assistant to the Director of the New Orleans Museum of Art, and Kurt, Vice-Chairman of its Board, are truly responsible for this first exhibition. They convinced us that the public would indeed be very interested and introduced us to the Museum's Director, E. John Bullard and the Curator of Decorative Arts, John W. Keefe, both of whom enthusiastically endorsed the idea of a public exhibition and an ensuing national tour. Once again, these beautiful objects have led us to interesting new friends and colleagues.

As with all collections, certain acquisitions become special favorites, due in part to the particular taste of the collector and sometimes a result of the circumstances surrounding their discovery. Such is the case with the five examples of Cartier flowers in this exhibition. Always considered a Fabergé specialty, representational carved stone flowers are rare in the work of Cartier. My particular favorite is the delicate Morning Glory (catalogue number XXXV); supported in a lifelike manner by an elegant ivory pole, it is the essence of refinement in its handsome Japanese-style pot; no detail has been overlooked; even a moonstone dewdrop has fallen to the ground. The graceful carved agate heron with his tall chased legs (catalogue number XXIV) is very much a part of the same spirit that inspired the flowers, and he too is unique to this collection. The unusual and elegant agate, gold and enamel cigar case bearing the double eagle crest of Imperial Russia (catalogue number XXV) is so appropriate to our particular household. Such a luxurious creation for a single cigar, it is as beautiful to behold as it is to touch. Within the *oeuvre* of Cartier, perhaps none of these singled-out favorites is of equal importance to the Mystery clock, acknowledged to be the *summa* of Cartier's output; however, it is these simple yet beautiful objects and others like them that charm and delight us every day, each with its own particular appeal. Living with these beautiful treasures has enchanced our lives immeasureably. We are proud to share our pleasure with a wider audience and to further the understanding and appreciation of the art of Cartier design.

Frayda B. Lindemann
New York City
August 5, 1988

THE LINDEMANNS AS COLLECTORS

I became fascinated by Cartier works of art in the 1970s. By the early 1980s, I had decided to specialise exclusively in this field. Knowing of our keen mutual interest in this subject, a friend had arranged for George Lindemann and me to meet in New York in May of 1985. I remember being whisked to the top of a skyscraper and into a smart modern office with amazing panoramic views over the city. It was decorated with communications equipment and photographs of show-jumpers and polo players. I was not sure what to expect but George was at once keenly inquisitive about Cartier, the diversity of the early works, the state of the market and availability of pieces. Every known catalogue and book was strewn over his desk. We struck up an instant and easy rapport. He was in a particularly good humour as he had recently acquired the important "Mandarin Duck" Mystery clock (catalogue number LXIV). "I saw the Mystery clocks first in the window of Cartier in rue de la Paix, Paris," George says, "I knew immediately I had to acquire an example." I instantly recognised a kindred spirit as George explained he was interested in collecting the splendid *objets d'art* made by Louis Cartier as well as better known jewellery. It always amazes me that while the name Fabergé is on the tip of everyone's tongue, Cartier as an *objets d'art* maker is almost forgotten. There is no doubt history will regard them in an equal light in years to come. "As a child," George explains, "and for many years thereafter, I collected watches and clocks. After I was married, I started buying jewellery for my wife and on a visit to Cartier in Paris saw for the first time the Mystery clocks. They were fascinating and this started us on the road to this collection." Frayda shares equally George's fixation for Cartier. They both have a highly developed sense of taste and style, and one of the immense charms of this collection is that it has been created by them both. Frayda says, "George and I sometimes differ on very specific matters of taste but we hardly ever differ at all about the collection as a whole. We love it the same way and we appreciate it the same way. We do however, have our individual favourites. I am particularly fond of the 'Comet' clock (catalogue number LIX) and the *chinoiserie* Siberian jade casket (catalogue number XXXVIII)." Shortly after our first meeting the Lindemanns acquired the first of many pieces through me, the Cartier cigar tube (catalogue number XXV), perfect for the cigar-loving George. More and more, we were in cahoots over long-distance telephone lines discussing the merits of the various pieces they had picked out at the auctions. I found myself hopping on and off planes in distant lands seeking out pieces which we had heard a whisper of. I like to think my knowledge has sometimes been helpful to George and Frayda. Often they have been able to go with greater determination after certain pieces while passing up others, safe in the knowledge no finer examples exist. At their insistence, only pieces in excellent condition are added to the collection. I remember the moment they discovered the small round enamel compact (catalogue number XLVI) in such perfect condition that the original powder pat was still inside unused. So detailed is their interest that it was not long before George and Frayda had discovered the entire history of powder makers! Likewise, not long after they had acquired the *chinoiserie* flower vase (catalogue number XXXVII), Frayda was excitedly on the telephone with the information that this was one of thirty vases commissioned by the Baron Armand de Rothschild as Christmas presents in 1928. They gain particular pleasure when something unusual or rare is found. For Frayda the most exciting find was the tall Morning Glory in the agate and sapphire pot (catalogue number XXXV). "I have always admired the Fabergé flowers," Frayda explains "but I was totally overcome when I saw the magnificence of this flower by Cartier. It was so totally unexpected. The way the stem rises up entwined with the ivory 'bamboo' pole. It is incredibly wonderful." The discovery of the two Cartier frames (catalogue numbers XXVIII and XLI) was also memorable but I especially remember when Frayda asked if I could find anything Cartier made incorporating an obelisk. It was her son's birthday and he was fascinated by obelisks. I knew Cartier made Obelisk clocks but had no idea how to find one.

Frayda asked me to try, adding that her son's birthday was in two weeks! It was an impossible mission but not a day later, quite by chance, in the back of a modern jeweller's, I stumbled on the Obelisk clock here exhibited (catalogue number LV). It made me think that perhaps this collection is meant to be. All these shared experiences have been great fun. George and Frayda have become close friends of mine and we have enjoyed some amusing and frustrating times. I have grown to respect their taste and integrity and am sure Louis Cartier would have been pleased by what they have achieved. Thanks to the extraordinary efforts of George and Frayda Lindemann the glory that once was Cartier is again revealed.

The Honorable Harry St. C. Fane
Director, Obsidian, London

THE LINDEMANNS AND CARTIER

Note:

This major contribution to the catalogue was in the course of preparation when Mr. Nadelhoffer's unexpected and untimely death occurred on July 28, 1988. This left many crucial issues unresolved. Rather than alter any of the original thoughts of Mr. Naddelhoffer, the world authority on the House of Cartier and its *oeuvre*, the Museum has elected to add comments it has deemed necessary in grey type. In this way, we hope the reader will be able to distinguish with ease the concepts defined by Mr. Nadelhoffer from those expressed by the Curator of the exhibition.

John W. Keefe

For far too long, the creations of the House of Cartier tended to be viewed as expensive ephemera having more to do with costume and fashion than with genuine aesthetic merit. A decade ago, few curators would have been taken seriously had they favorably compared the Mystery clocks of Cartier to the imperial Russian Easter eggs of Fabergé. However, this is now a generally accepted comparison, and current auction prices for the few Mystery clocks which become available publicly give no evidence of diminishing. Not only has recent scholarship altered the view toward the *oeuvre* of this great jewelry house, but conceptions internationally about jewelry have shifted. Until recently, the most prestigious antique shows in the United States did not acknowledge period jewelry as admissible genuine antiques or as a legitimate branch of the decorative arts. All that has, of course, changed radically within the past several years. Certainly, fine jewels in the Art Deco have recently come to be regarded as something beyond "estate" jewelry.

Today the discerning collector of Cartier's work has many varied avenues to explore. While Cartier's retrospective market has never competed with that of Fabergé in numerical terms, the past few years have seen a tremendous resurgence in dazzling *objets d'art* and jewels carrying the prestigious signature of the rue de la Paix. It is clear that this belated recognition of Art Deco has been born of a generation of connoisseurs whose predecessors turned a blind eye to the quality workmanship of the 1920s and '30s.

Unfortunately, much of the jewelry from this period was unappreciated and cruelly broken up some fifteen to twenty years later in favour of more contemporary styles. However, the decorative *objets d'art* with their definite shapes and eyecatching colours survived and remain as monuments to what is arguably Cartier's greatest period. Though many lay forgotten in safes and bank vaults they were rediscovered by a generation with a love of the *Ballets russes* and the '20s world of F. Scott Fitzgerald. Since the early 1970s the market for these pieces has proved stronger and stronger yet, and the myth of the Cartier *objet d'art* has slowly evolved.

In their selective approach to the works of Cartier, George and Frayda Lindemann have made use of an aesthetic flair which must have been inherent from generations past. Although it is true that a few items were already in George's parents' possession the core of what the New Orleans Museum proudly displays today reflects the couple's own distinguished taste.

The collection is based on two focal points: the clock, proud testimonial to the functional aesthetics of the firm, and the flower, quintessential *objet d'art* with *fin-de-siècle* appeal. While George Lindemann's passion for the world of the mechanical added one highlight after another to his range of timepieces, Frayda, with her love for the organic, the animal and the floral, developed a keen eye for the few Cartier flowers on a sparse market. These flowers are possibly Cartier's most rarified species. Two lilies-of-the-valley (catalogue number

XXXIV), a lily with sadly drooping flowerhead (catalogue number XXXII), a hyacinth (catalogue number XXXI), and a carnation (catalogue number XXXIII) fill Cartier's "dainty hot-house", appropriately cased in glass shrines which add a touch of architectural grandeur. Pride-of-place undoubtedly belongs to a unique Morning Glory, ten inches high (catalogue number XXXV), delicately supported by an ivory stick and created of almost colourless frosted rock crystal, chalcedony, and moonstone; shimmering pastel materials which evoke the world of the most delicate Chinese watercolours. The tub, with its strict rectangular latticework, exemplifies the taste of Art Deco and clearly distinguishes this item as an artifact of the 1920s. A pair of jade cacti (catalogue number XXXVI), the Mexican desert plant, which so attracted artists and interior decorators in the 1920s and 1930s goes further still in boldly sculptured abstraction.

The Cartier flower, made to conform to the aesthetics of the 1920s, admittedly had its roots in the work of the craftsmen of St. Petersburg, owing a debt to the supreme art of Fabergé. We know that in one instance the Cartier brothers bought a cornflower from Fabergé which was studied and analysed in their Paris workshops for refining to the tastes of their European clients. These included such demanding patrons as J. P. Morgan, King Alfonso XIII of Spain, and Lady de Grey.

Cartier's flowers were born out of the imagination of some gifted craftsmen, anonymous even today, who worked in the compound of Berquin-Varangoz's workshop at Saint-Siméon outside Paris. From 1918, Aristide Fourrier took control, employing 25-30 skilled staff members. It is obvious that Fabergé's dainty "Japanese" grouping of flowers with its still-life effect was particularly studied and convincingly rendered by this team. Most popular in this context was the amusing combination of the flower with a grasshopper or other insect, adding movement to the basically static flower with the odd falling leaf or drooping calyx evoking a melancholy state of transient decay. In rare examples the animal prevailed in size, as in the tiny sculpture of a philosophical heron on rock crystal ground (catalogue number XXIV) which combines such varied materials as agate, jade, lapis-lazuli, diamonds, and gold. The floral element, a waterlily, is clearly relegated to the background, while a frog is happily unaware of the imminent danger of the enemy.

Possibly the most popular image of the animal world, two love-birds perched side-by-side (catalogue number XXIII), was exemplified by numerous ashtrays and small sculptures. Love-birds, emblematic to Marie-Antoinette who was particularly fond of Venus's doves, are first registered in the rue de la Paix archives as early as 1881 in the form of brooches. Their appeal is clearly undimished a full century later.

In bold contrast to the flower, both in its monumental shape and striking colours, emerges the Cartier clock. The importance of the collection rests on the dazzling presence of six rare Mystery clocks, which conceal the surprise they contain as subtly as did Fabergé's Easter eggs. Their "surprise" is purely mechanical and creates the optical illusion of a seemingly rotating pair of hands; in reality they remain statically bound to separate glass discs, a technical *tour-de-force* which escapes the beholder's eye. Cartier owed the exclusive invention of the Mystery clock to the genius of a brilliant inventor, Maurice Coüet (1885-1963), raised in the best tradition of the Breguet school. As from 1912 he invented the exquisite series of "Comet" or "Planet" (catalogue number LIX) semi-mystery clocks, the year after his first Mystery clock saw the light of the day. Coüet surrounded himself with a team of designers who cased his clocks in daring shapes and in the most alluring colours of the mineral world. The first model, cubic in shape, and true to Art Deco principles, worked on the basis of a pair of symmetrical, lateral axles hidden to the eye, which rotate the discs. This model was continued for decades and is represented in the Lindemann Collection by an example dated to the outset of the Second World War (catalogue number LX).

Coüet's inventive urge soon transcended the bi-axial system of the first model by transmitting the mechanical impetus through a simple central axle. This inevitably gave rise to new shapes and structures; the *Ecran* model of rectangular tablet outline was born (1922). The collection contains a brilliant example in coral, mother-of-pearl, and rock crystal which proudly bears the initial of the present owners (catalogue number LXII), and also a further delightful single-axle model with octagonal rock crystal bezel dated 1921.

In 1925 Cartier placed the *Ecran* model into the daring context of a *garniture de bureau* (catalogue number LXIII), approaching the best that eighteenth-century French craftsmanship could have produced. Here in this superb agate, rock crystal, and coral-coloured enamel clock which graced for many years the writing desk of one of India's foremost Maharajahs a perfect blend of the functional and the aesthetic was achieved. A design recently discovered on the international market attributes the composition to Alexandre Diringer (born 1892) who joined Cartier at the age of 17 to remain for a further 17 years. From 1922, Diringer assisted watch-maker Joseph Vergely to design his clocks.[1] The present example is one among few with regard to firm evidence of attribution.

The paucity of designers' names attached to specific works in the Cartier *oeuvre* is occasionally frustrating and due in part to Louis Cartier's desire to keep the secret of such major pieces as the Mystery clocks away from his competitors. Early in its existence in New York, Cartier found that its New York competitors were only too willing to rush into production designs first seen at the Cartier Paris shop and thereby place them on the market before Cartier could import them to the United States. The desire for secrecy was accompanied by an equally adamant conception of Louis Cartier, and that was that *everyone* worked for the House of Cartier. So strong was his feeling for the overriding importance of "the House" that individual designer's names were frequently not recorded. It is clear that Cartier did not feel these to be as important as the firm itself. Indubitably, distinguished designs were filtered through the Cartier brothers or through the formidable Jeanne Toussaint (1887-1978) all of whom made suggestions and alterations, feeling little compunction to contact or credit the design's originator. Given this phenomenon, it is unlikely that we will ever know more about certain of Cartier's operations.[2]

Louis Cartier's own genius is best illustrated by a small series of animal clocks exemplified in the Lindemann Collection by the "Mandarin Duck" Mystery clock of 1922 (catalogue number LXIV), which was formerly in the possession of the Abdy family. It was usual for Cartier to incorporate exotic Chinese sculptures in bold harmony with the drum-shaped clocks, some portraying the weird and gruesome features of the fabled Far Eastern Chimera. However, the Lindemann piece displays a more placid subject altogether, impressive in size and stylishly carved by the late eighteenth or early nineteenth-century Chinese artist. Louis Cartier's eagle eye discovered these birds and animals on the art market prior to handing them over to his workshops to transform them into these startling timepieces.

The quintessential *tour-de-force* in the range of the Mystery clocks is the "Portico" model. Of the six in existence, five have found their final niche in private collections. The Lindemann model of 1924, surmounted by an enthroned Buddha (catalogue number LXV), transmits the mechanical impetus from the roof down to the clock. Suitably it blends Far Eastern architectural design within the aesthetic framework of the '20s. Here a pinnacle of the Art Deco mode is reached with a perfect balance of shape, material, and colour.

No Cartier collection is complete without hinting at the parade of the exotic *objet d'art:* the Egyptian, the Persian, and, above them all, the *chinoiserie.* Cartier's green and blue color combination had its antecedents both in the Egyptian and in the Indo/Persian context; a delicate vanity case of lapis-lazuli coloured enamel and greenish mother-of-pearl tiered borders (catalogue number XL) clearly refers to both. Lacquered *chinoiserie* which Louis Cartier again used to spot with unerring accuracy were placed, with indefinable taste, in the best Art Deco colour context. This is aptly demonstrated by an exquisite black lacquer vanity powder compact (catalogue number XXXIX); the scintillating colours of the Chinese scene are emphasised only by the most subtle cabochon sapphire and amethyst border; such is the restraint and discipline of the Cartier designer who respects a genuinely accomplished masterpiece from the past and gracefully raises it into the context of a new artistic dimension.

This ability to deal giftedly with antique elements and to lift them from their original context without destroying their integrity is surely one of the most salient indicators of the design quality achieved by the House of Cartier. Former opinions would have held that Cartier was merely a contributor to an already established jewelry style, the Art Deco; however, current scholarship and recent discoveries have clearly indicated that Louis Cartier and his colleagues were, in fact, major exponents and developers of the French Art Deco style. These revelations have also shown that Cartier made such a contribution at a far earlier date than had originally been thought. Thus one has two major elements to consider when dealing with the "Golden Era" years of the firm, *circa* 1919 through 1939; one, significant design and stylistic developments and, two, virtuoso craftsmanship which was almost unrivalled.

Hans Nadelhoffer
Jewelry Department
Christie's International, S.A.
Geneva, Switzerland
May, 1988

John W. Keefe
Principal Curator of Decorative Arts
New Orleans Museum of Art
August, 1988

NOTES:

[1]Alexandre Diringer worked for Vergely at the workshop of Maurice Couet in the rue Lafayette, Paris. (see Nadelhoffer, H., *Cartier: Jewelers Extraordinary,* Harry N. Abrams, New York, 1984, p. 249)

[2]Although the Cartier worksheets frequently name the particular *atelier*—Coüet, Bako, Lavabre, Fourrier—we do not as yet know a great deal about the specialties provided by each. For example, Maurice Coüet organized a Cartier workshop in 1919 at 53 rue Lafayette and hired freelance lapidaries such as Fourrier of Saint-Siméon; yet we know little specifically about what Fourrier supplied to Coüet while knowing that his shop (Fourrier's) was largely responsible for the fabrication of the rare Cartier floral groups. Similarly, we know that the Bako shop supplied fine enamels to Cartier, but almost nothing is known about individual enamellers within that *atelier.*

CHRONOLOGY OF CARTIER JEWELLERS

1847	Louis-François Cartier (1819-1904) lays the base of the first Cartier shop at 29 rue Montorgueil, Paris.
1853	Louis-François Cartier moves to more fashionable quarters at 5 rue Neuve des Petits Champs.
1859	Cartier moves to 9 boulevard des Italiens.
1859	Empress Eugénie de Montijo, spouse of Napoléon III, places her first order with Cartier for a silver tea service.
1871	Louis-François Alfred Cartier joins his father's business.
1871-1873	Cartier & Fils opens a temporary branch in London.
1874	Alfred Cartier succeeds his father.
1891	Installation of electricity.
1898	Installation of telephone.
1898	Louis-Joseph Cartier (third generation) becomes an associate of his father.
1899	Cartier, Paris, moves to present location at 13 rue de la Paix.
1900	First use of platinum.
	As early as 1853, this precious metal, already known in ancient Egypt, is mentioned in Cartier's archives. However it took fifty years to find a suitable alloy to replace oxidizing silver for use in setting pregious stones: a technical achievement which was also an aesthetic revolution.
1902	Cartier, London opens at 4 New Burlington Street.
1904	Queen Alexandra commissions her *resillé* necklace from Cartier in London.
1904	Royal warrant by King Edward VII.
	Through 1939, fourteen royal warrants were granted:
	1904 King Alfonso XIII of Spain
	1905 King Carlos of Portugal
	1907 King of Siam
	1909 King George of Greece
	1913 King Peter of Serbia
	1914 Duke of Orléans
	1919 King Albert I of Belgium
	1920 King Victor-Emmanuel III of Italy
	1920 Prince Albert of Monaco
	1921 Prince of Wales
	1928 Queen Marie of Rumania
	1929 King Fuad of Egypt
	1939 King Zog of Albania
1906	Jacques-Théodule Cartier (third generation) becomes manager of Cartier, London.
1906	Louis and Pierre Cartier become associates in Cartier, Paris.

1906	Appearance of first Art Deco jewels set with *calibré* gems.

At the turn of the century, two opposing trends ruled jewellery design. The goldsmiths, or orfèvres, subscribed to the Art Nouveau style in which assymetrical forms with soft lines inspired by nature were created using new materials, such as horn, ivory and celluloid synthetics. The jewellers, joailliers, of whom Louis Cartier was the leader, instead favored the revival of the elegant Louis XVI style. With a negative attitude towards Art Nouveau jewellery, he moved naturally from the geometrical patterns of the "garland" style to more linear designs. The records show that he encouraged his designers as early as 1906 to use calibré stones in the ornamental patterns which eventually lead to the later Art Deco style.

1907 Mrs. Evalyn McLean, an American, purchases the "Star of the South."

Many historic diamonds were sold by Cartier:
"Star of the East"
Blue "Hope"
"Blue Heart"
"Queen of Holland"
"Porter Rhodes"
"Nassak"
"Cumberland"
"Tigereye"
"Jubilee"
"Vega"
"Burton-Taylor-Cartier"
"Louis Cartier"

1907 Cartier's first exhibition in St. Petersburg at the Hôtel d'Europe.
It was inspired by the Paris exhibition of Russian art organized by Diaghilev in 1906.

1908 Cartier opens a temporary branch at 28 Quai de la Cour in St. Petersburg in competition with Peter Carl Fabergé.

1908 Grand Duchess Vladimir becomes Cartier's client.

1909 Cartier, London moves to 175-176 New Bond Street.

1909 Charles Jacqueau joins Cartier as their foremost designer.
His many sketchbooks, cahiers d'idées, *were frequently adopted from the* Gazette du bon ton *and from visits to exhibitions and museums, mainly the Louvre. But his greatest impressions translated into jewellery come from Diaghilev's* Ballets russes *where his dancers, Nijinsky, Karsavina, Rubinstein, Pavlova...who were dressed in oriental costumes moved through sceneries designed by Léon Bakst as in Rimsky-Korsakov's colorful "Sheherazade." The still fashionable pastel shades were replaced by striking joyful colors.*

1911 The first "Santos" watch was created for Louis Cartier's friend, the Brazilian aviator Alberto Santos-Dumont (1873-1932).

1912	First appearance of the baguette cut.
	This invention of a style of step-cutting, mainly for small diamonds, is attributed to Louis Cartier. It found its application principally in the geometric designs of the late Art Deco jewellery.
1912	The Paris City Council presents a Cartier Easter egg to Tsar Nicholas II.
	The competition with Fabergé is in full course.
1913	Creation of the first "Model A" Mystery clock, sold to the American tycoon-banker J. P. Morgan.
1917	Cartier, New York moves to its present location at 633 Fifth Avenue.
	The Morgan Plant Building was acquired in exchange for a double row necklace of natural pearls.
1919	Creation of the "Tank" watch inspired by the Renault armoured cars of the Allies in World War I.
1920	Technical improvement of the Mystery clock.
1922-1931	Creation of twelve "Chinese" Mystery clocks with carvings of the nineteenth century:
	1922 "Jade Mandarin Duck"
	1924 "Agate Chimera I"
	1925 "Two Jade Carps": with a dial of the concept of Grollier de Servières (not a Mystery Clock)
	1925 "Jade Vase and Bird Flower"
	1925 "Crystal Turtle"
	1925 "Agate Chimera II" with round citrine dial.
	1926 "Chinese Goddess Kuan Yin"
	1927 "Crystal Chimera"
	1928 "Jade Elephant"
	1929 "Jade Buddhist Lions"
	1930 "Coral Chimera"
	1931 "Jade Chimera Goddess Kuan Yin": movement with striking chimes.
1923-1925	Creation of six "Portico" Mystery clocks:
	1923 Dodecagonal dial in crystal with "Billikin," the Anglo Saxon Buddha-like "God of the underworld and of plenty."
	1924 Octagonal dial in crystal with square pillars.
	1924 Dodecagonal dial with square rose quartz pillars and two Buddhist lions.
	1924 Dodecagonal dial in crystal with Buddhist lion (head to the right).
	1924 Dodecagonal dial in crystal with Buddha.
	1925 Dodecagonal dial in crystal with Buddhist lion (head to the left).
1924	First advertising of the famous three color gold "rolling rings" and bracelet.
1925	Louis Cartier is appointed a member of the jury at the Paris *Exposition Internationale des Arts décoratifs et industriels modernes.*
	This event gave the name, Art Deco, to the period of early twentieth-century art.
1929	Cartier opens a branch in St. Moritz, Switzerland.

1931-1986	Creation of twenty-six presentation swords for French Academicians. *The* Académie Française, *an association organized by Richelieu in 1634 to foster the French language, edited the great dictionary. Dissolved at the Revolution, it was reconstituted in 1794, as part of the* Institut de France. *Since Napoléon's time, the forty members respect dress regulations supplemented with a sword, reflecting their work, which is presented by friends and admirers.*
1933	The patent for the invisible setting of stones registered: *serti mystérieux*.
1933	Jeanne Toussaint (1877-1978) becomes a *Directrice de la Haute Joaillerie*. Described by Sir Cecil Beaton as "a woman of bird-like stature," she was not a designer herself, but endowed with a sixth sense of taste.
1938	Cartier opens a branch in Cannes.
1940	Cartier, Paris, transfers operations to Biarritz during the German Occupation. *Cartier's also moved their archives temporarily to London for safekeeping. While the workshop there produced intricate parts for aircraft and cameras and created the Cross of Lorraine's emblem to be worn with the uniform of the Free French Forces, Cartier's London board room was held at the disposal of General de Gaulle for meetings and to pronounce his statement on BBC on June 18, 1940.*
1945	Jacques Cartier (fourth generation) becomes director of London branch.
1945	Pierre Cartier becomes president of Cartier International.
1946	A brooch, originally designed by Jeanne Toussaint, as a bird in a cage, secretly symbolizing the German Occupation, was re-designed to disclose the secret by showing the little bird singing at the opened door of the cage, to celebrate the Liberation.
1948	Claude Cartier (fourth generation) heads Cartier, New York.
1948	Creation, for the Duchess of Windsor, of a panther brooch with cabochon sapphire of over 150 carats, by Jeanne Toussaint. *Nicknamed "the Panther," she inspired many successive and successful creations, promoting this elegant animal which appeared for the first time in a watch in 1914, to become the symbol of Cartier.*
1962	Claude Cartier sells Cartier, New York.
1964	Marion Cartier sells Cartier, Paris.
1972	Joseph Kanouï heads a group of investors who acquire Cartier, Paris.
1972	Robert Hocq becomes president and Alain Dominique Perrin marketing manager.
1973	Creation of *Les Must de Cartier* with openings in Biarritz, Singapore, and Tokyo.
1974	Cartier takes control of Cartier, London.
1976	Another group of investors acquires control of Cartier, New York and appoints Joseph Kanouï as chairman.
1979	Merger of Paris, London, and New York groups create Cartier World.
1983	Creation of the Cartier Foundation for Contemporary Art on Juoy-en-Josas, near Versailles.
1983-1984	Cartier, Geneva, assembles the Musée Cartier collection from its affiliates in Paris, London, and New York.

Eric Nussbaum,
Director, Musée Cartier
Geneva, Switzerland

THE HOUSE OF CARTIER AND THE LINDEMANN COLLECTION

It is probable that Louis-Francois Cartier (1819-1904), the founder of the House of Cartier, never dreamt that his jewelry firm would continue into the late twentieth century as one of the most celebrated and esteemed in the world. Certainly Louis-Francois had been an able and astute businessman, for his modest firm, opened in 1847, was a mere twelve years later supplying jewels and luxury goods to the most exalted names of the French aristocracy and to the Empress of France, the fashion-plate Eugénie, who in 1859 placed her initial order for a silver tea service. The acumen of the founder was inherited by his son Alfred (1841-1925), who succeeded him in 1874. Alfred handled the sale of some of the most celebrated jewelry collections of the era, thus spreading the fame of the Cartier enterprise far beyond the environs of Paris.[1] However, it was Alfred's three sons, Louis (1874-1942), Pierre (1878-1963) and Jacques (1884-1942) who took over the already-prestigious family business and built it into an empire which dominated the European jewelry trade, both monetarily and aesthetically. As had been earlier the case with the Russian court jeweler, Peter Carl Fabergé, the three Cartier brothers were conducting the right business at the proverbial right time in the right places. In 1867, the first major diamond had been discovered in South Africa[2]; the African diamond fields soon supplanted the traditional sources of Brazil and India. The French pavilion at the Philadelphia Centennial Exhibition of 1876 drew the favorable attention of affluent Americans, thus setting the stage for the arrival slightly later of the fabulously rich "robber baron" American multi-millionaires.[3]

Just two years later, the great Paris exposition of 1878 firmly established the hegemony of French decorative arts worldwide. By the turn of the century, the riches of colonial possessions were pouring into Europe, and the "Age of Opulence" was well established. Newly rich bankers, speculators and financiers on both sides of the Atlantic sought to emulate the lifestyles of the old aristocracy. The large diamonds made available by the African mines were avidly sought, and the economically privileged indulged themselves in the pastime of publicly displaying their wearable, portable wealth. The House of Cartier elegantly encouraged this with its "garland" style *(style guirlande)* and was available to supply as well such expensive fripperies as golden yo-yos,[4] ivory and gold swizzle sticks, and gold toothpicks, the last for King Farouk of Egypt. Just after the turn of the century, Cartier was producing a major tiara a week. As the rich of the Western world flocked to the marble portals of Cartier, so did titled and crowned heads; from 1909 through 1939, the firm received no less than fifteen letters patent appointing it the official purveyor of jewels and *objets de vertu* to such royal households as those of England's Edward VII, Russia's Tsar Nicholas II, Italy's King Victor-Emmanuel III, Romania's Queen Marie and King Chulalongkorn of Siam. This august patronage did not, however, deflect the enterprising Cartier brothers' attention from their solid trade with the less visible *haute bourgeoisie* of the world and, indeed, with the entire spectrum of society. The actress Lillie Langtry was a famous Edwardian client (1902)[5] as was the celebrated "Grand Horizontal", Caroline Otéro, (1903) and the Islamic religious leader, the Aga Khan (1903). The French aesthete and author Marcel Proust traded at Cartier's (1910) as did celebrated Parisian couturier Jeanne Lanvin (1922).

Until 1917, such clients shopped with fabled leading members of the soon-to-fall Russian aristocracy. During the 1920s and 1930s, Cartier attracted the trade of the Indian potentates and maharajahs; the Oriental splendor of the taste of such figures as Gaekwar of Baroda, The Nizam of Hyderabad and the maharajahs of Indore, Nawanagar and Patiala threatened to outstrip that of the House's most freespending Western world patrons. Jeweled crowns, diamond necklaces, elaborate *toilette* sets, pearl collars and a plethora of jeweled objects were regularly ordered by these Eastern aristocrats. At the same time, the late Duke and Duchess of Windsor, the American heiress Barbara Hutton and, later, the actress Elizabeth Taylor were important Cartier customers. The diversity of patrons and objects purveyed notwithstanding, all of the Cartier clientèle had a common denominator, and that was limitless wealth. Not uncommonly, this wealth was accompanied by an equally refined taste; herein lies the artistic importance of the House of Cartier. While some of these patrons indubitably only desired something appropriately expensive, Cartier never let down its standards of excellence and was simultaneously capable of producing an opulent object as well as one which possessed aesthetic merit.

If the period of 1900 to 1917 marked years of triumph for the House of Cartier, by the 1920s the brothers had established a veritable empire. Although close, the three men were of different temperaments, which made their accomplishment all the more remarkable. Pierre was, perhaps, the most at ease in the world of business; as such, he was the ideal family member to head the New York branch, which had been founded in 1909 on New York's exclusive Fifth Avenue. Eight years later it was the persuasive Pierre who convinced the socialite Mrs. Morton Plant and her husband to trade a palatial neo-Renaissance residence at 635 Fifth Avenue for a double strand of Oriental pearls. The mansion was speedily and tastefully converted into a series of *soigné* showrooms, which retained an aura of their former residential function, and remains the New York premises of Cartier. Pierre readily adapted to his position as a transplanted Frenchman and eventually married an American. The New York branch initially imported its wares from the rue de la Paix store but was soon able to set up its own smithing and lapidary shop, which meant that it could turn out French-inspired designs quickly. This was an important consideration since many newly affluent customers in the United States were firmly convinced that anything of merit must come ultimately from Paris, and Cartier's New York competition was not above rapidly copying Parisian designs and marketing them before the recently founded New York branch could import its own wares.

The youngest of the brothers, Jacques, was the most sensitive and least outgoing of the three. In 1901, his father, the astute Alfred, opened a London branch in order to cater to the English aristocratic and mercantile trades; five years later, Alfred officially withdrew from an active role in the business, leaving Pierre and Jacques in charge of the London office. Pierre's departure for New York in 1909 put the youngest son in full charge in London. Jacques was to maintain this position through the 1919 split with the rest of the House of Cartier; during the 1930s, European political events dictated that the London branch acquire a greater independence in matters aesthetic; the shy Jacques skillfully handled this modification while steadily accruing a valuable new patronage with the Indian princes and maharajahs.

However, of the three sons of Alfred, it was the eldest, Louis, who was to have the major impact upon the House of Cartier in the twentieth century. That rare combination of keen appraiser of market trends, aesthetician and collector, Louis had entered the Parisian office in 1896 at the age of twenty-one. It was he who began to change the Cartier image as a dealer in an expensive welter of bronzes, silver flat and hollow wares, antique furniture, Sèvres porcelain, ivory cabinet figures and, of course, jewelry. His father, Alfred, had presided over the premises thus stocked during the heyday of the Second Empire (1852-1871) and had even made original contributions to the jewel trade.[6]

However, it was young Louis who was to direct the primary focus of the House of Cartier to important jewels and objects. Notably cool to the contrived lyrical charms of the new Art Nouveau style,

Louis elected to pursue, through the *fin-de-siècle* and early years of the present century, the "garland" style for which the House was then acclaimed. As a serious collector of French eighteenth-century paintings and furniture, Louis was able to translate these superbly designed and crafted objects into jewelry recalling the splendors of the eighteenth-century French court. Simultaneously, of course, such jewels also directed themselves to the courtly pretensions of the period's newly affluent. Such a vogue had really been created by the Second Empire Empress Eugénie, who had had her jewels spectacularly remounted in the style of Queen Marie-Antoinette; in 1887, these celebrated pieces (by now the possession of the French government) were sold at auction. Included were a bowknot with pendant tassels and a pair of shoulder bowknots. Louis Cartier was quick to see that this taste could readily be reworked to suit contemporary preference, since costume required tiaras, body jewelry (including corsages and stomachers), dog collars and ropes of pearls.[7]

The "garland" style evolved by Cartier was, in essence, a revival of the taste of the Louis XVI (reigned 1774-1793) period and favored a regal kind of symmetry and balance; in short, it was a style admirably suited to the formality of the period. The diamonds which were the primary stone of the style were held in flexible platinum settings which themselves had been finished to scintillate and sparkle, thus enhancing the gems they held.

Louis Cartier was to remain as astute a judge of fashion and shrewd marketing when the formal symmetry of the "garland" style began to disappear. By 1910, the ostentatious stomacher was rendered obsolete by the disappearance of the shaped bodice under the influence of such *avant-garde* designers as Paul Poiret. These ponderous mementoes of *la belle époque* were usually intrinsically so valuable, however, that they were broken up and subsequently fashioned into smaller, more modish

pieces of jewelry. Some of Cartier's most exuberant and expensive designs are only known today through the firm's practice of carefully preserving original sketches and design drawings (see the finished gouache drawing for the unique standish incorporating an *Ecran* Mystery clock, page 33, now in the Lindemann Collection, catalogue number LXIII.). This was not an unusual practice for many of the world's leading jewelry houses. However, time and unfavorable political events have destroyed many of these. The House of Cartier would appear to be unique in its preservation of a number of original designs for objects, many of which have long since been broken up and incorporated into pieces bearing little or no resemblance to the original conception. The House of Cartier has also preserved a large number of the original work sheets which meticulously list for whom a piece was made and on what date. These work sheets frequently contain as well a list of the materials used, sometimes noting the fact that some of the gems to be utilized had been brought in by the owner. As such, they form a fascinating history of patronage of a distinguished jewelry firm.

If the stomacher disappeared due to changes in dress design, the once-ubiquitous tiara had been, by the outbreak of World War I, largely relegated to use at official, ceremonial court functions. It need not be emphasized that there were few official courts remaining in Europe at the termination of the Great War. A less formal but no less effective replacement for the tiara was the aigrette, a long gem-set hair ornament which terminated in a fetching spray of osprey feathers. Cartier was to become a major purveyor of these and of *bandeaux*, browbands which were requisitely expensive and chic but nowhere near as cumbersome to wear as the tiara.

However, as stated by the late Hans Nadelhoffer in his brilliant pioneering book on the history and products of the House of Cartier, Louis Cartier's greatest role was to be played in the development of the Art Deco style.[8]

As a collector of Islamic art, Louis Cartier travelled to India and became familiar with the flat pierced, trellis-like patterns of Moghul art as well as with its frequently brilliant polychromy. The influence of Indian color coincided with the astonishing palette introduced by the *Ballets russes* which had first appeared in Paris in 1909. In this, the pale evanescent colorings of the Art Nouveau manner were superseded by vivid contrasts of brilliant blue and green, shimmering blue and purple, dramatic red and black. Both of these influences, as well as the searing colors of *Fauve* (Wild Beast) paintings, inspired Cartier to produce glistening enamelled surfaces combined in an unorthodox manner with the cold glitter of cut gems and the glow of such hardstones such as jade, onyx and coral. Indifferent as he had been to the Art Nouveau style, young Cartier was nonetheless influenced by the emerging Cubist school of painting from which he took geometric motifs and adapted them as decorative ones. These, in turn, were combined with the Islamic lattice and star motifs with which he had earlier experimented. Even before absorbing all of these influences, Cartier had been impressed by the superlative enamels of Fabergé, and these, too, were carefully studied and absorbed into the new Cartier mode. This fashion was later shaded by the 1922 discovery of Tutankhamun's tomb and the resultant craze for *égyptérie*[9] and by the exoticism of Chinese art; all of these elements were successfully grafted by Cartier onto his own version of the Art Deco style. This manner successfully combined the arts of the Orient with the linear geometric stylizations of the reigning European designers.

This important contribution to the Art Deco style was accompanied by an equally cogent and compelling philosophy which dictated that jewelry had to be both contemporary *and* functional. This led inevitably to an immense array of objects in-tended for daily use such as smokers' articles, vanity and lipstick cases, multipurpose boxes, clocks and desk accessories. No matter how mundane their function, these articles were exquisitely crafted of the finest metals, enamels, hardstones and gems.[10] No object seemed too trivial to warrant the fullest of Cartier's painstaking attention to detail and superlative ornament.

Although the inquiring mind and eye of Louis Cartier led him continually to expand his range, it was in the realm of clocks and watches that his "functioning jewelry" reached its zenith. In 1904, at the request of the Brazilian aviator Alberto Santos-Dumont, Cartier developed a wristwatch the observation of which would not require the aviator's taking his hand away from the airplane controls. From this was born the wristwatch of today which generally replaced the traditional pocket or case watch. In 1919 the renowned Tank watch was designed with a profile which recalled the American tanks which had been so instrumental in aiding the defense of France in World War I. It is today regarded as the most classic of wristwatch designs.[11]

Six years earlier, in 1913, the firm had produced its first Mystery clock *(pendule mystérieuse)*, in which a faceted hardstone dial contained diamond hands which kept the time without visible works. The Mystery clocks were all executed for Cartier by the atelier of the remarkable Maurice Coüet (1885-1953), the descendant of a line of clockmakers whose collaboration with the House of Cartier was to be one of the most productive and inventive of the firm's history. Coüet was a knowledgeable admirer of antique timepieces by such celebrated French makers as Nicolas Grollier de Servières (1593-1685/86) and Robert-Houdin de Blois (1805-1871). He was also fascinated by illusionistic devices within the dial of a timepiece. This fascination, coupled with his admiration and knowledge of complex period movements, led Coüet to develop the "Comet" or "Planet" clock (catalogue number LIX) around 1912. Many horological historians regard this as a forerunner of the fully developed Mystery clocks, which appeared only a year later. The first Mystery clock was entitled "Model A" (catalogue number LX), and it is generally considered by jewelry historians to have ushered in the "Golden Era" of the House of Cartier, circa 1919 to 1939. These Mystery clocks are to the House of Cartier what the imperial Easter eggs were to the Russian House of Fabergé.[12] The architectonic "Model A" Mystery clock was followed by five different types of Mystery clocks, each of which, however, had variants within its type. The second model, created in 1920 (catalogue number LXI), possessed a rather more exotic form, that of a hexagonal faceted hardstone dial framed in enamel with a diamond bezel set upon a rectangular base. The base of these models was generally fabricated of onyx and bore golden Chinese-style bracket feet. So popular was this model of Mystery clock that it had nineteen variations by 1931.

The third Mystery clock model was the *Ecran* (screen) of 1923 (catalogue number LXII). The inspiration of this form was apparently a Louis XVI or First Empire style firescreen, long a fixture in *grand luxe* suites of French furniture and a form which would have been well known to Louis Cartier in his role as a collector of antique French decorative arts. By 1928, seven variants of the *Ecran* clock had been carried out, and the firm continued its production until 1954. Significantly, the Lindemann's collection includes two of the *Ecran* Mystery clocks, a standard coral and onyx model and one in which the *Ecran* clock is uniquely incorporated into a sumptuous agate, rock crystal, diamond, enamel, and gold standish (catalogue number LXIII). Originally owned by an Indain maharajah, this is a splendid example of Cartier's brilliant eclecticism.

In 1920, Cartier's and Coüet had introduced a pendant dial clock in the form of a Chinese gong which appeared to keep time without any visible mechanism. By 1923, the pendant dial concept had been sufficiently refined to produce the first of the famous "Portico" Mystery clocks (catalogue number LXV). These took the form of Oriental gateways and featured a central pendant dial operated by a central axle system concealed in the lintel of the gate. The first "Portico" model was received with great acclaim, and five others were produced by 1925.

Roughly contemporary with the "Portico" models were the elaborate figure or *animalia* Mystery clocks, which comprised a fifth category of the mystery types. Like the *Ecran* models, these twelve clocks had their inspiration in the *pendules à sujets* of the Louis XV and Louis XVI eras in which the clock movement rested on the backs of horses, rhinoceri, elephants, and bulls. However, their relationship to eighteenth-century prototypes ended here, for the figural supports of the *animalia* series were selected antique Oriental objects which had been lifted out of their period context and subtly reworked by the Cartier workshops. Thus the "Mandarin Duck" clock (catalogue number LXIV) whose base is actually a simple very early nineteenth-century Chinese jade duck has become a stylish ruby-studded Art Deco pedestal for an equally contemporary dodecagonal topaz dial and chapter ring.

Significantly, as mentioned elsewhere in this publication, George Lindemann had earlier begun to collect antique European clocks and watches, an interest which he generally pursued alone as the subject was not one of overwhelming interest to his wife. However, on a trip to Paris in the late 1970s, the Lindemanns first saw Cartier's Mystery clocks.[13] Subsequent to their purchase of Cartier earrings in 1981 (catalogue number I), Eric Nussbaum, Curator of the Musée Cartier in Geneva, Switzerland, transported the "Mandarin Duck" Mystery clock to New York for the Lindemanns to inspect. This famed clock was the first (1922) of the Cartier *animalia* series, and both of the Lindemanns knew that it had to become part of the collection. In this fashion, the highly important Cartier clock is also a sort of keystone of the entire collection, since it happily united both of the couple's interests and set them off on a collecting adventure which has become one of mutual pleasure.

Although the Mystery clocks have captured the public imagination since their introduction, it should be pointed out that the House of Cartier continued to produce other fine clocks and watches throughout the period. The "Prism" clock by Gaston Cusin was introduced in 1937 and reintroduced in 1984. The firm also experimented with electric wristwatches. That elegant arbiter of taste, Jeanne Toussaint (1887-1978), Louis Cartier's friend and advisor, who watched over the firm's designs for decades, became increasingly involved with clocks following 1937. Although she herself never actually designed an object, her ideas and favored motifs often inspired successful Cartier designs; the popular "Three Turtles" table clock of 1962 was a Toussaint inspiration.

In terms of strict chronology, however, the Lindemann's collection began in 1981 with the purchase of the aforementioned pair of diamond and pearl pendant earrings (catalogue number I) fabricated by Cartier about 1918. These combined elements of both the established "garland" style and of the emerging geometric Art Deco mode. This acquisition was significant for it was Frayda Lindemann's first important purchase at Cartier, and stylistically the earrings presaged the Art Deco flavor which enhances the entire collection. In terms of the history of the House of Cartier, these earrings were an appropriate acquisition, for pearls remained a major category of jewelry at Cartier's through the 1920s, accounting for sixty percent of the firm's sales. So important were they that pearls were shown to clients in a specially designed room.

Louis Cartier was not amused by the development of the Japanese cultured pearl industry and scornfully referred to that product as "white beads." What began as a straightforward purchase for evening wear sparked the imagination of the Lindemanns as a couple, and was the first step toward the assembling of what many critics and connoisseurs regard as the finest collection in the United States of Cartier jewels and objects.

Stylistically, the Lindemann Collection concentrates on pieces produced by the House of Cartier during the so-called "Golden Era" years of *circa* 1919 through 1939. Both collectors responded instinctively to Cartier objects of this period which were virtually unrivalled for design and craftsmanship internationally.

The Second World War was indubitably the single greatest crisis faced by the House of Cartier. In the early 1930s, the long-established fashion for jewels set in platinum had come to an end, and yellow gold re-entered the fashion arena. However, by 1940, its wholesale trade was forbidden by the *Banque de France;* this led to a series of experimentations with gold alloys and, in New York, with palladium, not even then recognized in France as one of the "noble metals." The firm, however, did not succumb to the tribulations of the War, but it was certainly not an era of lavish spending for luxury items. In 1942, both Jacques and Louis Cartier died; with them went the firm's great inspired Art Deco designs. Neither brother had been particularly comfortable with the emerging Art Moderne style. Not until the 1950s had the world sufficiently recovered economically to shop once again at Cartier. The tenacity of the firm however, had been hinted at with the 1948 order of the Duchess of Windsor for a "panther" brooch; this was followed in 1956 by the Duchess' purchase of a "tiger" bracelet (catalogue number XVII). A stylized "panther" pelt motif in *pavé* diamonds flecked with onyx had entered Cartier's design repertoire as early as 1914. However, it was Jeanne Toussaint, one of whose favored motifs was a panther, to conceive of a "Great Cat" series in the late 1940s. The trendsetting Duchess of Windsor's commissions were followed in 1957 by those of the Princess Nina Aga Khan, and five years later, by the American heiress Barbara Hutton.

Although the Lindemanns' collection continues into the era of the "Great Cats" series, both responded best to Cartier's production between the two World Wars. While acknowledging their positive response to objects whose most common stylistic denominator was that of the Art Deco, neither ruled out the aquisition of pieces whose dates fell before or after the "Golden Era" years. Thus, the collection has come to include Late Victorian and Edwardian clocks and objects of adornment as well as the diamond "Tiger" suite at the opposite end of the date range. However, certain rules were set for the collection. Pieces were to possess a "sculptural presence," by which term was indicated a strong three-dimensional character which allowed a particular piece—no matter how small—to function as an autonomous sculptural object. This preference, of course, was very much in accord with Louis Cartier's personal predisposition to the architectonic. Above all, any object to enter the collection had to have visual appeal; it was not to be a collection assembled solely for investment or speculation purposes. Materials and their use were certainly to be considered, but design was the issue. Should a nephrite object work more successfully than a diamond-enframed emerald one, the former example was to be acquired.

Like many collectors, the Lindemanns found that their horizons broadened rapidly and soon encompassed not only jewelry and clocks, but *objets de vertu*. The initial earring acquisition was followed by lipstick and cigar cases, paper knives, clocks and other timepieces, hardstone sculpture and the rare floral groups. It is interesting to note

that once George and Frayda Lindemann had decided to concentrate upon creations of the House of Cartier, George's mother Lilyan Lindemann, presented the couple with a handsome jeweled enamel lipstick-vanity case (catalogue number XLV) and the elegant Art Deco gentleman's evening watch (catalogue number LIV) which had originally belonged to her husband, Joseph S. Lindemann. Both of the new collectors began to read voraciously, became avid readers of sales catalogues and attended the major international auctions. It was at this time that they became acquainted with such leading authorities on the House of Cartier as Hans Nadelhoffer whose major book on Cartier had gained him world recognition.[14] They also came to know the leading purveyors of Cartier goods and other collectors of Cartier; in short, like earlier specialized and dedicated collectors, they found an unexpectedly expanded circle of interested persons opened to them.

The feelings which the Lindemanns had initially—and continue to have—for these rare and precious objects were, of course, exactly these which Louis Cartier and his brothers had sought to arouse in discriminating clients. These were not merely objects of fashion crafted for a moment's pleasure but *objets de vertu* and examples of the goldsmith and lapidary arts which would withstand the crucial test of history. How right Louis Cartier had been to feel that his were significant timeless and classic creations and how astute the Lindemanns' acumen in perceiving this.

Assuming the Cartier contention, adapted from the philosophy of Peter Carl Fabergé earlier, that all materials are equally valid for use in an art object is correct ... and that unorthodox combinations of these materials are justified, provided the final result is a pleasing composition ... one can readily see how the creations of the House of Cartier have come to be viewed as authentic art objects. Certainly one of the criteria by which an *objet de vertu* passes from the realm of fashion into the mainstream of the history of the decorative arts is that it speak eloquently of its time and place. In the process of creating genuine art objects, the House of Cartier had helped to forge the tenets of a new style, that of the international Art Deco, a movement presently universally accepted as one of the major stylistic trends of the early twentieth century. The passage of time has patently indicated that the overwhelming majority of the creations of the House of Cartier reflect their period as engagingly and as validly as the treasured jewels of the Renaissance or the gold and gem-set eighteenth-century European snuffboxes so highly esteemed by the collectors of the late twentieth century.

John W. Keefe
Principal Curator of Decorative Arts
New Orleans Museum of Art

NOTES:

A version of this essay, entitled "Reflections of Elegance: Cartier Jewels from the Lindemann Collection," was originally published in *Arts Quarterly*, the house publication of the New Orleans Museum of Art, Volume number X, issue 4 for October, November, and December of 1988. Its purpose here is to give the reader of this catalogue a general overview of the history of the fabled House of Cartier, a history which will complement the primary catalogue essay of the late Hans Nadelhoffer and the excellent chronology contributed by Eric Nussbaum, Director of Cartier *Haute Joallerie*, Geneva Switzerland, and Curator of the Musée Cartier in that city.

[1]In 1871, the famous courtesan and hostess, La Barucci, sold her splendid jewels through the Cartier firm. This was but the beginning of a series of transactions by the firm on behalf of the owners of important jewel collections. The House of Cartier eventually handled the sale of pieces for such illustrious owners as the exiled Prince Felix Youssoupov, other members of the Russian nobility and the Habsburg Dynasty of Austria.

[2]The perfect metal with which to complement the glitter of diamonds, platinum, had been discovered in the Urals in 1822. It came to greater and greater use in the late nineteenth century since it, too, possessed a brilliant lustre, was eminently malleable and did not oxidize as silver did.

[3]The House of Cartier was the primary source of important jewels for such prominent American families as Astor, Goelet, Gould, Leeds, Morgan, Vanderbilt and Widener through the 1930s. Fortuitously, Louis Cartier had married Andrée-Caroline Worth, granddaughter of the renowed couturier Charles Frederick Worth (1825-1895), in 1898, thus allying two of the leading luxury trade businesses of the world. Persons of fashion ordering clothes from the House of Worth at number 7 rue de la Paix had only to go to Cartier at number 13 in order to enhance their sumptuous costumes with fitting jewels.

[4]W. K. Vanderbilt of New York was a major customer for these yo-yos.

[5]The years cited here are the first of a Cartier purchase for each of the persons named.

[6]The semiprecious "tiger's-eye" had been launched in Paris in 1882; a year later Cartier offered a pair of earrings featuring the new stone. During this period, Alfred Cartier also introduced Paris to English Victorian-influenced jewelled brooches in the form of salamanders, turtles and butterflies.

[7]This assortment left little room for necklaces of large composition, and long sleeves had temporarily eclipsed the major bracelet.

[8]Nadelhoffer contends that Louis Cartier began to experiment with the Art Deco style as early as 1906. Art Deco was to emerge as the major international style at the famous *Exposition Internationale des Arts décoratifs et industriels modernes* held in Paris in 1925.

[9]The Lindemann Collection includes a small exquisitely crafted lipstick case in the form of a canopic jar in the Egyptian taste. Its inlay of turquoise and lapis lazuli recalls the colouration of early Egyptian faïence.

[10]In 1929, Louis Cartier opened "Department S" (for Silver), a progenitor of today's *Les Must de Cartier*, which sold "affordable" objects and fashion jewelry.

[11]Both the Santos and the Tank watch remain in production by Cartier World today.

[12]Cartier had, in fact, produced an Easter egg for presentation to Tsar Nicholas II in 1912. It is now in the collections of the Metropolitan Museum of Art, New York.

[13]During this trip, the Lindemanns viewed among others, the important "Jade Carp" Mystery clock and an example of the "Portico" Mystery clock which are both in the collection of the Musée Cartier, Geneva, Switzerland.

[14]Sadly, Mr. Nadelhoffer, one of the essayists for the major catalogue which accompanies this exhibition, died in Geneva, Switzerland, in July of this year. This tragic and untimely event terminated the distinguished and ongoing pioneering research he was conducting on the House of Cartier.

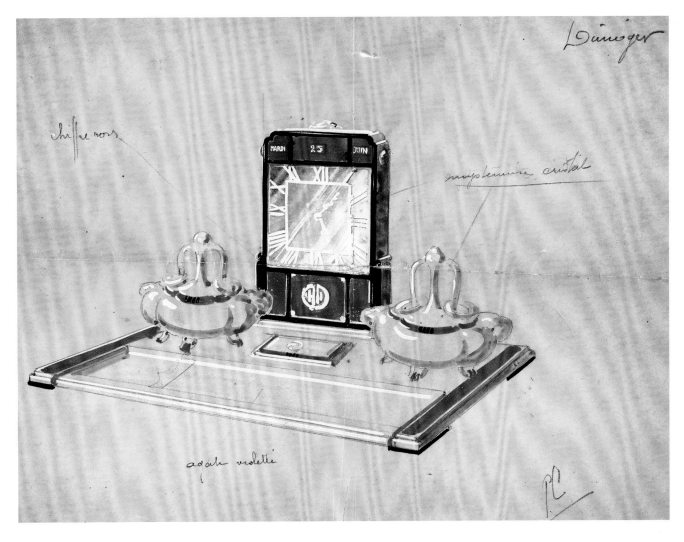

Alexander Diringer (born 1892)
Study for *Ecran* Mystery Clock and Standish,
gouache and pastel, 1925.

Photograph courtesy of Hans Nadelhoffer,
Christie's International, S.A., Geneva, Switzerland

    This elegantly finished design drawing for the *Ecran* Mystery
clock Standish is by Alexander Diringer who was one of Maurice
Coüet's (1885-1963) most talented protégés, having entered his
workshop as a teenaged boy. Diringer was assigned to the clockmak-
ing department of the Coüet *atelier* in 1922.

    The fact that this finished drawing is signed by Diringer may in-
dicate that he was its designer. Although Cartier retained many
highly detailed drawings for its designs, the majority of them are unsigned due to Louis Cartier's insistence on the predominance of the
House of Cartier over the designs and names of individual artisans.

    For further comments on this drawing, see page 19.

JEWELS AND OBJECTS OF ADORNMENT

PLATE I

PAIR OF EARRINGS

Diamond, pearl, and platinum.
circa 1918.

L. 2³/₄"
L. 7cm.

Each earpiece is a diamond *pavé*-set fleur-de-lys from which depends a flexible chain of alternating circular diamonds and diamond *pavé*-set rectangular links terminating in a large pearl of 13.50 millimeters.

Fabricator: Cartier, New York.

Cartier Stock Number: #24-70018.

Provenance: Cartier, New York.
            The Lindemann Collection, New York, from 1981.

Comments:

Platinum had been used only tentatively in jewelry during the second half of the nineteenth century, but became increasingly popular after the turn of the century. The metal permitted flexible, lacy settings, which imparted a remarkable delicacy to the designs in which it was utilized. This characteristic became extremely important as adornments decorated with many genuine gems gained in social acceptablity, and after the discovery of the South African diamond mines in the 1860s made quality gems much more plentiful.

The combination of large lustrous natural pearls and diamonds came into international vogue during the 1880s and remained so until just after World War I. Indeed, pearls constituted sixty per cent of Cartier's trade through the late 1920s. The business in natural pearls flourished in spite of the incursions of the Japanese cultured pearl industry. Fashionable jewelers referred to the new Japanese pearls scornfully as *boules blanches*, or "white beads."

In this century, the House of Cartier is best known for its Art Deco designs. However, this distinctive style evolved through many phases. In many ways, these earrings represent a subtle transition between the end of the century "garland" style and the Art Deco mode. While the diamond and pearl combination, pendant drop form, and Louis XVI iconography distinctly define these jewels as products of the *belle époque*, the attention to contrasting textures and overall geometric simplicity presage the Art Deco taste.

These were the first Cartier objects purchased by the Lindemann's (1981) and mark the beginning of their collecting interest.

PLATE II

BROOCH

Diamond, onyx, rock crystal, and platinum.
circa 1925.

Ht. ⅞" W. 2¾" D. ⅛"
Ht. 2.2cm. W. 7cm. D. .3cm.

Designed in the Art Deco style, this brooch is composed of a central rock crystal rectangle lined with *pavé*-set rose and baguette diamonds. The crystal is joined on either end with *pavé*-set rose diamond bands to gabled terminals. These motifs are executed in parallel rows of *pavé*-set rose diamonds; the outer of larger gems than the inner row. The area inside the diamond bands is mounted with black onyx and set with three marquise, and two rose diamonds.

Fabricator: Lavabre Workshop, Paris, for Cartier, Paris.
Cartier Stock Number: #A 01454.

Provenance: Mr. and Mrs. A. C. Humphreys, Jr.
Charline H. Breeden.
Auction: Christie's, New York,
April 12, 1983, #308, illustrated.
The Lindemann Collection, New York,
from 1983.

Comments:

The House of Cartier justly enjoys a distinguished reputation for fine jewels in the Art Deco style. Possibly because of Louis Cartier's personal reticence to embrace fully the Art Nouveau style with its flowing organic lines, the transition from the "garland" style to mature Art Deco designs was relatively quick for the firm. Although Cartier experimented with typically Art Deco elements as early as 1906, it was not until after World War I, when general social upheaval produced a taste for the unconventional and dramatic, that such designs became widely popular. In keeping with his philosophy that jewels and fashions were interdependent, Louis Cartier began producing the designs which complemented contemporary wardrobes, and, today, are considered definitive examples of Art Deco taste.

In creating these designs, Cartier geometrically simplified many of the basic shapes of the "garland" style, and exchanged its subtle color combinations for bright contrasts. In this brooch, the contrast of softly glowing rock crystal juxtaposed with the glittering brilliance of diamonds and onyx aptly suited the tenets of Art Deco taste. Such a juxtaposition of stones admirably illustrates Louis Cartier's contention that all materials are valid, provided the result is harmonious.

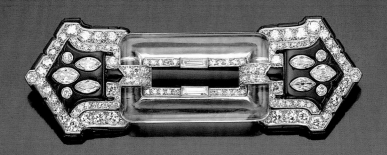

PLATE III

HANDBAG

Coral, diamond, enamel, gold, and *peau de soie*.
circa 1925.

Ht. 5³/₈″ W. 8⁷/₁₆″ D. ³/₄″
Ht. 13.7cm. W. 21.4cm. D. 1.9cm.

A flat rectangular clutch bag covered in black *peau
de soie*. A twist clasp is composed of a pyramidal
coral boss mounted on a gold plaque. The square
mount is black enamel on gold with triangular-
shaped *pavé*-set rose diamond corners.

Fabricator: Cartier, Paris.

Cartier Stock Number: None.

Provenance: Cartier, New York.
The Lindemann Collection,
New York, from 1982.

Comments:

The handbag became a popular fashion item in
the 1920s. Its immediate predecessor, the vanity or
nécessaire, was a small case usually made of metal
that was equipped with several small storage compartments. Although such cases were popular
throughout the 1920s, the materials from which
they were constructed necessarily limited their
size. With the advent of cosmetics and increasing
tolerance of public smoking, women required more
space than was feasible in the vanity. The popularity of the handbag owes a great deal to its ability to
provide a lightweight and capacious alternative that
also appealed to the Art Deco penchant for
function.

Around this time, Louis Cartier (1875-1942) in
collaboration with his great friend Jeanne Toussaint
(1887-1978) and talented designer Charles Jacqueau (1885-1968), was creating the famous "Department S." Originally the "S" stood for silver, but
under the direction of this collaboration it retailed
an assortment of functional items. Here the sophisticated client could find everything from ashtrays
and fashion accessories to letter knives and desk
sets. Virtually nothing was beyond receiving the
Cartier treatment.

Over the years, from 1925 on, handbags were a
part of the "Department S" inventory. These exquisite and useful objects were accomplished in
styles which complemented the fashions of the day.
Stylishly ornamented in gems, hardstones, and precious metal, this elegantly simple clutch bag well
represents the Cartier philosophy of the "functional
jewel."

Louis Cartier had early advocated the use of materials whose colors and textures boldly contrasted;
certainly the glowing salmon-pink hue of the
opaque coral functions well against the lustrous
black enamel and discreetly glittering diamonds.
This combination was frequently employed by the
Cartier in both jewelry and *objets de vertu* as well.

For further comments on the evolution of the
handbag as a fashion accessory, see catalogue numbers V, IX, X, XIV, and XVI.

PLATE IV

HAT CLIP

Onyx, emerald, diamond, and platinum.
circa 1925.

L. 3½"
L. 8.9cm.

Designed as an onyx annulus, bearing at each side a rose diamond and onyx *pavé*-set striped band linked to arrowhead form terminals. The arrowheads are also *pavé*-set in cushion shaped diamonds and *calibré* onyx and emeralds. Each is centered with a larger cabochon emerald, and further enchanced with pierced geometric designs.

Fabricator: Cartier, Paris.

Cartier Stock Number: Unknown.

Provenance: Auction: Sotheby's, London, December 11, 1986, #371, illustrated. The Lindemann Collection, New York, from 1986.

Comments:

In the transition to the Art Deco mode, Cartier retained many of the elements of the earlier "garland" style. Simplified with a new geometric awareness, the curvilinear forms of the tassellated and bowknotted garland manner were adapted. Yet, for the apparent geometrization the new Cartier designs consistently display qualities which reveal the inspiration from individual plants or fruits.

The circle, as here, and the ellipse, derived from earlier wreath forms, were principal Cartier Art Deco shapes. In Cartier Art Deco designs these were often further modified with stylized terminals which elongated the form to appeal to the new taste. In this instance, an important and stylish clip was created to suit ideally the bell-shaped cloche hats fashionable during the 1920s. Its startling contrasts of translucent emeralds, glittering diamonds, and glowing opaque onyx were characteristic of the most sophisticated Cartier designs of the period.

A similar form, is illustrated in a line drawing in: Nadelhoffer, H., *Cartier: Jewelers Extraordinary*, Harry N. Abrams, New York, 1984, p. 187.

PLATE V

HANDBAG

Diamond, sapphire, emerald, enamel, gold, and
lizard skin.
circa 1925.

Ht. 4½″ L. 7¾″
Ht. 11.5cm. L. 19.8cm.

A rectangular-shaped white lizard evening bag
with accentuated gold hoop enamelled in black.
The cylindrical hinges are *pavé*-set with rose diamonds, and further enhanced with plume-like borders executed in rose diamond and *calibré*
emeralds. The clasp reiterates the diamond plume
decoration and is accented with an emerald bead
topped by a cabochon sapphire.

Fabricator: Unknown.

Cartier Stock Number: None.

Provenance: Auction: Sotheby's, Geneva,
May 15, 1985, #535,
color illustration, plate XCIV.
The Lindemann Collection,
New York, from 1985.

Comments:

In "Department S", Cartier's handled a variety of
luxurious functional items. Handbags, which came
into vogue during the 1920s, were a part of its inventory. While some were simply adorned, others
were fabulously appointed with gems set in current
fashionable motifs. Originally covered in black
suede, this bag with its Indo-Islamic-inspired
adornment complements a whole range of Cartier
accessories.

Such Indo-Islamic motifs were a major contribution of Louis Cartier to the formulation of the international Art Deco style. An avid collector of
ancient and eastern art, Louis Cartier's interests in
many ways mirrored those of his contemporaries
who were attracted and mesmerized by the exoticism and opulence of these foreign cultures. With
his usual acumen, Louis Cartier began retailing

jewelry and objects of antiquity. However, his most
important accomplishment was the integration of
non-European elements into his own designs.

In this handbag, the synthesis is evident in the
choice and treatment of the gems and adornment.
The sapphire and emerald combination and plume-
like decoration are reminiscent of Moghul jewelry.
Derived from the exquisite enamels of Lucknow,
the capital of the Indian province of Oudh, the blue
and green combination was a Cartier favorite. Combined with black, and often pink, it became a perfect expression of the Art Deco style. The
adornments have undergone a similar change in
their transformation from the Indo-Islamic palm
design to the simplified and elongated geometric
diamond arrowhead motif popular in Cartier Art
Deco designs.

This unusual handbag is also an exquisite example of Cartier's mechanical inventiveness. Beau-
tifully adorned, it is foremost practical. Its sleek
profile is comfortable for carrying, while the deftly
crafted cylindrical hinges allow the hoop to open
into a wide polygonal shape for easy access.

For further comments on the evolution of the
handbag as a fashion accessory, see catalogue numbers III, IX, X, XIV, and XVI.

PLATE VI

BROOCH

Diamond, rock crystal, enamel, and platinum.
circa 1926.

Ht. 1⅝" W. 3⅝" D. ⁷/₁₆"
Ht. 4.1cm. W. 9.2cm. D. 1.1cm.

The brooch is composed of rock crystal rectangle lined with *pavé*-set, rose and European-cut diamonds, and joined on either side to pyramidal elements by *pavé*-set diamond bands bordered in black enamel; the pyramidal features are both platinum and *pavé*-set with rose diamond borders terminating in a pear-shaped diamond. A larger European-cut diamond is claw-set in the square open space of each motif. They are further enhanced with delicate black enamel geometric patterns.

Fabricator: Unknown.

Cartier Stock Number: #1259.

Provenance: Miss Amelia Peabody, Boston.
Auction: Sotheby's, New York, April 22-27, 1985, #162, illustrated.
The Lindemann Collection, New York, from 1985.

Comments:

Cartier followed the established precedent of utilizing older stones belonging to clients and reworking them into currently fashionable designs. Art Deco taste particularly favored the contrast of the soft sheen of rock crystal against the brilliant glitter of diamonds and opaque black enamel.

For further comment, see catalogue number II.

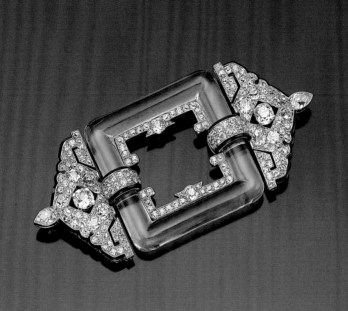

PLATE VII

BRACELET AND JABOT PIN

Diamond, onyx, coral, and platinum.
circa 1927.

Bracelet: L. 7¹/₄″
           L. 18.4cm.
Pin: Ht. ³/₄″ W. 2¹/₄″ D. ³/₁₆″
      Ht. 1.9cm. W. 5.6cm. D. .4cm.

The bracelet is designed as a chain, consisting of carved "Figure 8" centers and linked with eight oval domed links *pavé*-set in diamonds interspersed with onyx cabochons. The pin is designed as a carved stylized coral palmette, the center and lower edge of the body are *pavé*-set in diamonds and alternating single and paired onyx cabochons. The terminal of the pin is *pavé*-set in diamonds and onyx to form a pendant loop the knot of which ends in a pendant coral fan.

Fabricator: Cartier, New York.

Cartier Stock Number: Bracelet: #11-70127.
                          Pin: #12-11138.

Provenance: Cartier, New York.
              The Lindemann Collection,
              New York, from 1983.

Comments:

The chaste yet bold juxtaposition of coral, onyx, and diamonds reflects the Art Deco stylistic preference for contrasting colors and materials. This had been influenced earlier by the revolutionary advances of the *Fauve* (Wild Beast) painters (1905) and the brilliantly colored stage sets of the *Ballets russes* which first appeared in Paris in 1909. The House of Cartier was an innovator in the fabrication of such elegantly simple designs; bold contrasts of color and texture were a specialty.

The use of this combination was the product of an inspired collaboration between Louis Cartier and Charles Jacqueau (1885-1968). Jacqueau joined the firm in 1909, and from then until World War I designed many particularly elegant objects in the "garland" style for Cartier. A remarkable talent, however, he was not satisified with the limitations of this mode. By 1925, he and Louis Cartier had amassed an inventory of work in the new style. This forethought gave Cartier a distinct artistic advantage over competitors when later this same year the predominance of the Art Deco style was established at the important *Exposition Internationale des Arts décoratifs et industriels modernes.*

PLATE VIII

BROOCH IN THE FORM OF A TEMPLE

Diamond and platinum.
1927.

Ht. 1³/₈″ W. ¹¹/₁₆″ D. ¹/₄″
Ht. 3.5cm. W. 1.8cm. D. .6cm.

This brooch is designed as an eighteenth-century *temple d' Amour.* It is comprised of four baguette diamond columns with *calibré* diamond capitals resting on a base of channel-set *calibré* and baguette diamonds. The pediment is constructed of baguette and fancy cut diamonds, and supports a *pavé*-set rose diamond dome. The dome terminates in a marquise and *calibré* diamond vane.

Fabricator: Cartier, Paris.

Cartier Stock Number:#12-70129.

Provenance: Madame M. L. Erstery.
Cartier, New York.
The Lindemann Collection,
New York, from 1983.

Comments:

The *temple d' Amour,* originally a Roman form, was revived in the Renaissance and later lifted by eighteenth century architects as a fashionable garden object. Queen Marie-Antoinette had such a folly erected on the grounds of the Petit Trianon. Considered one of the most classic of Cartier's Art Deco designs, it became a virtual logo for the House of Cartier from 1925 to 1935, providing the opportunity for a virtuoso display of diamond cutting. Such brooches were introduced at the Paris *Exposition Internationale des Arts décoratifs et industriels modernes* in 1925, and their fame spread quickly after attracting the interest and support of such notable individuals as Elsie de Wolfe.

Often inspired by buildings from antiquity and non-European models, columns, arches, pagodas,

and Taj Mahals as well as the *temple d' Amour* found expression in Cartier designs. Louis Cartier was extremely interested in the architectonic possibilities of his designs. Among the many innovations and inventions credited to the firm, is his creation of the baguette cut in 1912. According to Louis Cartier, this cut, combined with other fancy cuts, such as the *trillion,* and rhombus-shaped gems, provided designers with the neccessary "building stones" to create objects with a three-dimensional focus. Although the jewels of this particular series are relatively literal translations, the same philosophy was applied to designs which were not architecturally inspired.

For further comments and comparison, see catalogue numbers XI, and XII.

PLATE IX

HANDBAG

Tortoiseshell, gold, and linen.
circa 1925-1930.

Ht. 6"L. 9"
Ht. 15.2cm. L. 22.9cm.

A flat rectangular handbag/clutch combination covered in bone colored linen. The clasp is a pyramidal tortoiseshell boss set in a gold plaque surrounded with a lozenge-shaped tortoiseshell mount with bevelled corners, and pierced by a tortoise-shell peg attached to the mount by a fine gold chain. An oval tortoiseshell thumbpiece and rectangular link secure the adjustable strap.

Fabricator: Cartier, Paris.

Cartier Stock Number: None.

Provenance: The Lindemann Collection,
New York, from 1984.

Comments:

The relaxed social attitude of the 1920s and '30s advocated the espousal of such fabrics as linen, cotton, and muslin for day wear; these replaced the heavy sumptuous fabrics of the late Victorian era and the diaphanous embroidered laces and silks of the Edwardian epoch. This handbag admirably sums up this more flexible and comfortable attitude toward one's clothing and behavior. At the same time, its adjustable strap permits the bag to be worn in a variety of ways, a reflection of the Art Deco preference for objects having multi-functions.

The bag also reflects Louis Cartier's tenet that no object was too ephemeral or mundane to be treated in a refined aesthetic manner. The breadth of Cartier's range can be seen in his application of this concept to both jewelry and items of apparel.

For further comments on the evolution of the handbag as a fashion accessory, see catalogue numbers III, V, X, XIV, and XVI.

PLATE X

HANDBAG

Diamond, platinum, and silk
circa 1925-1930.

W. 6"
W. 15.2cm.

A rectangular-shaped black silk evening bag. The frame is platinum applied with black enamel, black silk and decorated with cylindrical hinges *páve-set* with rose diamond. The frame is further enhanced with a *páve-set* diamond clasp in a stepped geometric design.

Fabricator: Unknown.

Cartier Stock Number: None.

Provenance: Auction: Sotheby's, New York, 1987, #56, illustrated.
The Lindemann Collection, New York, from 1987.

Comments:

The handbag became an increasingly important fashion accessory during the 1920s; as usual, the House of Cartier made itself available to provide elegant examples of the form. Like the white lizard handbag (catalogue number V), this sleek and comfortable handbag is designed for practicality with the unusual hinge mechanism which is decorative while allowing easy access.

Non-European arts like those of India, Egypt, the Middle East, and the Orient played an important role in the development of Cartier's Art Deco style. Louis Cartier was particularly interested in Persian rug designs and the Mesopotamian ziggurat. In varied forms, elements of these images were translated frequently into Cartier designs. The Near Eastern influence is reflected in the stepped designs adorning the hoop of this handbag. Such simple and emphatically geometric shapes were popular during the second phase of the Art Deco mode.

It is accompanied by its original red leather fitted presentation case stamped Cartier.

For further comments on the evolution of the handbag as a fashion accessory, see catalogue numbers III, V, IX, XIV, and XVI.

PLATE XI

BROOCH IN THE FORM OF AN ARROW

Diamond and platinum.
circa 1928.

Maximum Ht. ⅝″ W. 2″ D. ¼″
Ht. 1.6cm. W. 5.1cm. D. .6cm.

The diamond-in-platinum mount brooch is designed as a stylized arrow. The body is formed as a truncated pyramidal tip of *páve-set* diamonds with a larger keystone diamond at the joint of the tip and shaft. The first is joined to another keystone diamond, and then to the terminal feathers and butt. These are a stylized plume-like device in *páve-set* diamonds which swirls around the end of a band consisting of a cushion, *calibré*, and fancy cut diamonds.

Fabricator: Cartier, New York.

Cartier Stock Number: #70056.

Provenance: Cartier, New York.
The Lindemann Collection,
New York, from 1983.

Comments:

The arrow shape was a favorite of the Art Deco style. Its simple geometry complemented the whole range of new tailored fashions. The organic treatment of this basic form is a trademark of Cartier's Art Deco designs. Such brooches, which permitted the display of various diamond cuts, became synonomous with the work of the firm after the great *Exposition Internationale des Arts décoratifs et industriels modernes* of 1925.

This brooch exemplifies not only Louis Cartier's architectonic interests, but his ability to assimilate elements of non-European art into his designs. The influence of ancient and eastern art is readily apparent in the pyramidal body, and the plumed terminal which resembles the Indo-Islamic palm design. The originality and uniqueness of the Art Deco mode owe a great debt to the vision of Louis Cartier and the ability of his designers to make this synthesis.

For further comment on Cartier's architectonic interest, see the Temple brooch, catalogue number VIII.

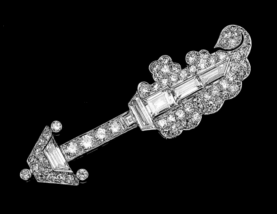

PLATE XII

JABOT PIN

Diamond, light canary yellow diamond, onyx,
enamel, and platinum.
circa 1930.

Ht. 1¹/₁₆″ W. 2¹/₄″ D. ¹/₈″
Ht. 2.7cm. W. 5.7cm. D. .3cm.

A diamond set platinum pin designed in the Art
Deco style. The stylized truncated palmette body is
pavé-set in rose diamond pierced and accented
with black enamel geometric designs. The setting
enhances a large pear-shaped light canary yellow
diamond in an onyx collet, and three square fancy
cut diamonds set at right angles to each other. The
design of the terminal repeats this motif with two
large square fancy cut diamonds accented with
black enamel geometric borders rimmed with *pavé*-
set rose diamonds.

Fabricator: Cartier, New York.

Cartier Stock Number: #12-11142.

Provenance: The Lindemann Collection,
New York, from 1983.

Comments:

Jabot pins became popular in the 1920s as lapel
ornaments and accents for the wide variety of new
hat styles. Cartier produced many such items in a
variety of forms. In these typically Art Deco designs, Cartier followed the established tenet of simplified forms with an emphasis on geometrization.

In contrast to many of his contemporaries, however, his inspiration invariably came from plant life
and incorporated elements of ancient, or non-
European art. The stylized palmette used in the
design of this pin was a favored Cartier motif

derived from numerous examples in ancient Egyptian and Indo-Islamic art.

Although the shape is indicative of Cartier's designs at this time, the combination of gems is unusual for Art Deco objects. The subtle contrast
between it and the rose diamond borders suggests
the central canary yellow diamond may actually be
a reset older diamond. Although the certainty of
this is unknown, the resetting of important jewels
from family heirlooms into new styles was fashionable in the Art Deco period.

For further comments, see catalogue numbers
VIII, and XI.

PLATE XIII

DOUBLE CLIP

Ruby, diamond, and platinum.
circa 1930.

Ht. 1″ W. 1¼″ D. ¼″
Ht. 2.5cm. W. 3.2cm. D. .6cm.

Each clip is designed as a platinum mounted
scroll. A *pavé*-set diamond swirl rimmed with *calibré* ruby extends from a paper-curl set with *trillion*
and baguette diamonds.

Fabricator: Cartier, Paris.

Cartier Stock Number: None.

Provenance: Auction: Christie's, New York,
April 12, 1983, #291, illustrated.
The Lindemann Collection,
New York, from 1983.

Comments:

In these clips, Cartier exhibits the full spectrum
of Art Deco tastes. Their simple flowing design and
bolder stylization which mark them as belonging to
the second phase of the mode admirably combines
the penchant for color and textural contrasts and
practical use with Louis Cartier's interest in architectonic qualities and adaptation of antiquarian
forms. While the scroll image is of ancient origin,
its rendering here in lustrous rubies and glittering
diamonds is a combination oriented to contemporary taste. The clips can be worn separately or
joined together to form a single scroll brooch; such
double function clips were extremely popular in the
later 1920s and '30s. At the time, the necklines of
many dresses called for the embellishment of a clip
at either side.

Simultaneously, the apparent layering of various
cut luxurious materials is a Cartier hallmark. The
juxtaposition of baguette, *trillion*, and *calibré* gems
in both *pavé* and channel settings accentuates their
three-dimensional quality.

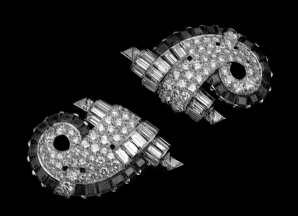

PLATE XIV

EVENING BAG

Diamond, onyx, gold, platinum, and crocodile.
circa 1930.

Maximum Frame W. 5½"
Maximum Frame W. 14cm.

A rounded bordeaux colored crocodile evening bag mounted in platinum and 18 karat white gold. The hoop, decorated in the "Panther" motif, is *pavé*-set with small diamond brilliants, and fancy shaped onyx spots.

Fabricator: Cartier, London,
(maker's hallmark, J.C.).

Cartier Stock Number: None.

Provenance: Auction: Sotheby's, Geneva,
May 15, 1985, #529,
color illustration, plate XCIII.
The Lindemann Collection, New York,
from 1985.

Comments:

During the late 1920s, the evening bag became a fashion imperative. Properly adorned, it provided the necessary accent to complete any ensemble. Although many of Cartier's designs were simply decorated, others display a full range of Art Deco tastes. This one, originally covered in black silk, is adorned in a favorite Cartier motif, the "Panther." In glittering diamond and lustrous black onyx, it exemplifies the taste for contrasting colors and textures.

The "Panther" motif first appeared on a pendant watch in 1914. During the Edwardian epoch, when specific styles and fabrics were strictly prescribed for various occasions, a very similar motif was used to complement mourning wardrobes. However, the theme was most notably revived in the late 1940s by Louis Cartier's great friend and collaborator Jeanne Toussaint (1887-1978) as part of the "Great Cats" series.

For further comments on the evolution of the handbag as a fashion accessory, see catalogue numbers III, V, IX, X, and XVI.

PLATE XV

PAIR OF CLIPS

Ruby, emerald, diamond, platinum, and white gold. circa 1930-1932.

Ht. 1⅛" W. 1" D. ¼"
Ht. 2.8cm. W. 2.5cm. D. .6cm.

Each clip is designed as a palmette. An intricate border is created with *pavé*-set rose diamonds in platinum. A carved emerald, and two carved rubies are held in the open center by delicate white gold mounts.

Fabricator: Cartier, New York.

Cartier Stock Number: None.

Provenance: Auction: Christie's, New York,
September 12, 1983, #294,
illustrated.
The Lindemann Collection, New York,
from 1983.

Comments:

Ardent innovators, Cartier designers continually added and varied elements in their Art Deco objects. Although the designs consistently reflect the popular geometrization, invariably the inspiration for them came from atypical sources. In contrast to his contemporaries Louis Cartier's forms were often derived from individual plants and fruits and non-European art; this pair of clips is an elegant example of this synthesis. The inspiration for these leaf-like clips is clearly Indo-Islamic.

Louis Cartier (1875-1942) was the originator of Indian-influenced jewels, having early been a collector of Indian art. His flourishing trade with the incredibly rich Indian potentates heightened his awareness of their art and, specifically, Moghul jewelry. From 1901, Cartier began integrating elements of Indian art into their designs. In these clips, the adaptation of Moghul taste is reflected by a vibrant juxtaposition of color and the use of carved emeralds and rubies.

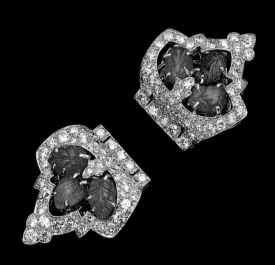

PLATE XVI

HANDBAG

Diamond, enamel, platinum, and suede.
1931.

Maximum W. 6"
Maximum W. 15.2cm.

A truncated pyramidal-shaped handbag with chamfered basal corners. The frame is covered with black suede. The hoop is articulated with a band of *pavé*-set diamonds and a double clasp of *pavé*-set diamonds with *calibré* channel-set diamond ends. A black suede handle strap is attached to the frame on either side by black enamel rectangular links joined with cylindrical *pavé*-set diamond bands.

Fabricator: Cartier, Paris.

Cartier Stock Number: #2810.

Provenance: The Lindemann Collection, New York, from 1984.

Comments:

The tailored form of this handbag matches perfectly the chaste but dramatic contrast of the *pavé*-set diamond hoop and clasp with the deep matte-black surface of the gathered suede. Cartier had early favored such bold contrasts in his jewelry and carried it over to fashion accessories.

The pronounced geometric character of the double clasp marks this piece as a product of the 1930s, a period during which chunky, forthright ornamental forms were preferred. As such, the clasp presages the Art Moderne style of the 1940s.

For further comments on the evolution of the handbag as a fashion accessory, see catalogue numbers III, V, IX, X, and XIV.

PLATE XVII

SUITE OF "TIGER" JEWELS

Canary yellow diamond, emerald, onyx, and gold.
Bracelet: 1973, Brooch: 1986, Earrings: 1986.

Bracelet: Ht. 2⁷⁄₈″ W. 2³⁄₄″ D. ³⁄₄″
       Ht. 7.4cm. W. 7cm. D. 1.9cm.
Brooch: Ht. 2³⁄₈″ W. 2³⁄₁₆″ D. 8⁷⁄₈″
      Ht. 6cm. W. 5.5cm. D. 22.5cm.
Earrings: Diam. ¹⁵⁄₁₆″
      Diam. 2.4cm.

This suite is designed in the "Tiger" motif. The annular bracelet and the brooch incorporate the likeness of the animal from which derives the name, while the penannular ear clips are simply striped in a tiger-like fashion. The stripes on all pieces are executed in gold *pavé*-set canary diamonds and cramp set baguette black onyx. The brooch and bracelet are further enhanced with pear-shaped emerald eyes and carved black onyx noses. The body of the tiger bracelet is hinged and clasps at the front paws. The languid body of the brooch is accentuated with a baguette diamond band.

Fabricator: Bracelet: Cartier, New York.
         Brooch: Cartier, Paris.

Cartier Stock Number: Bracelet: #015899.
              Brooch: #30039.
              Earrings: #30413.

Provenance: Cartier, New York.
         Cartier, Paris.
         The Lindemann Collection, New York, from 1985-86.

Comments:

"Great Cat" motifs appeared in Cartier's designs as early as 1914, but became most popular in the 1940s, '50s, and '60s. They were the inspiration of Jeanne Toussaint (1887-1978), Louis Cartier's great friend and collaborator. The brooch of the series was modeled on the celebrated imperial Austrian Order of the Golden Fleece. In contrast to the symbolic Art Deco designs, later works such as these became fantastic creatures based on realistic representations in which Cartier craftsmen captured the liveliness and vigor of the great cats.

Spotted motifs in diamond and onyx had appeared as a mourning motif in the Edwardian epoch, but it remained for Jeanne Toussaint who owned a Cartier panther-ornamented vanity case as early as 1917 to introduce a series of three-dimensional animals during the late 1940s. "Fantasy" animals such as the ones presented here were collectively known as the "Great Cat" series and soon attracted a broad international clientele, whose ranks included the Duchess of Windsor, the Princess Nina Aga Khan, and Barbara Hutton.

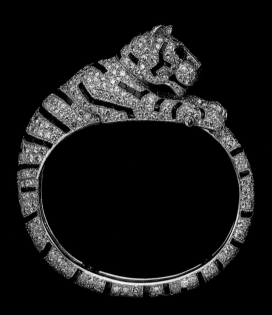
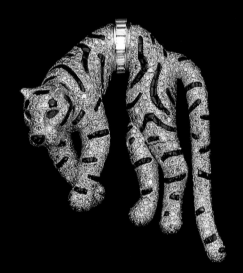

OBJETS DE VERTU

PLATE XVIII

BELL PUSH

Brown agate, sapphire, gold, enamel, and silver.
circa 1906.

Ht. 2 ⅛″
Ht. 8cm.

A carved translucent brown agate rabbit with cabochon sapphire eyes. The figure is mounted on a
short cylindrical base with gold bun feet. The base
is silver with turquoise *guilloché* enamel. The top,
in a sunray pattern, is rimmed with an opaque
white enamel border. White enamel bands encom-
pass the sides of the base. The side is enhanced
with an undulating gold foliate band.

Fabricator: Cartier, Paris.

Cartier Stock Number: #92.

Provenance: The Lindemann Collection, New York,
from 1988.

Comments:

Electricity was still an expensive novelty during
the opening years of the present century. The elec-
trically operated bell push thus became a diminutive status symbol used to summon distant
household servants. Bell pushes had been among
the most popular of desk and table top objects created by Peter Carl Fabergé (1846-1920), and the
Russian influence is evident here.

From 1904-1905 Cartier created a number of
such-inspired objects in response to the demands
of their Paris and London clients who were fascinated with distant Russia, and delighted by the
useful qualities many such objects presented. At
first purchased from Russian workshops, Cartier
began transfering the bulk of his orders to the Paris
ateliers of Bako, Fourrier, and Lavabre as they became expert in similar creations. They were never
able to duplicate the entire range of Russian enamels but did create many new colors and combinations.

Although many of the Cartier *objets de vertu* were
Russian-inspired, they were not slavish copies. In
the Paris workshops Cartier designers integrated
Russian elements with those of the "garland" style,
a revival of the Louis XV and Louis XVI styles
which was popular during the *belle époque*. This
synthesis is evidenced in this charming bell push
by the engaging Russian-like rabbit atop the circular base whose style and form recalls the *bonbonières* of the late eighteenth century, and is
decorated with the Cartier standard white enamelled bands and undulating foliage patterns subtly contrasted against the soft blue.

For further comments and comparison, see catalogue numbers XXIII and XXIV.

PLATE XIX

BELT BUCKLE

Diamond, gold, enamel, and platinum.
circa 1907.

Ht. ³/₁₆″ W. 2 ⁵/₈″ D. 2 ¼″
Ht. .4cm. W. 6.5cm. D. 5 .7cm.

An oval buckle in blue *guilloché* enamel decorated with borders of delicate rose diamond scrolls *pavé*-set in platinum. It is accented by rose diamond and platinum florets, located at the juncture of the buckle and clasp. The clasp, as well as the double tongue are fashioned of 18 karat gold.

Fabricator: Cartier, Paris.

Cartier Stock Number: #318.

Provenance: Mrs. Cornelius Vanderbilt, New York.
Auction: Christie's, New York,
April 15, 1986, #21, illustrated.
The Lindemann Collection, New York,
from 1986.

Comments:

Such prominent belt buckles were fashionable at the turn of the century when shirtwaists and skirts had become the rage under such influences as illustrator Charles Dana Gibson's "Gibson Girl." The delicate fleurettes and diamond bordering of this example recall the eighteenth-century French style of Kings Louis XV and Louis XVI. However, the buckle is by no means a copy of its inspirational prototype. Although the shape and enamelled surface are consistent with the earlier styles, as in many of Cartier's "garland" creations, the use of platinum and a quantity of genuine gems are distinctive of the *belle époque* taste.

A similar belt buckle is illustrated in: Nadelhoffer, H., *Cartier: Jewelers Extraordinary*, Harry N. Abrams, New York, 1984, plate 5; and in Gautier, G., *Cartier, The Legend*, Arlington Books, London, 1981, opposite page 96, lower.

COMB

Tortoiseshell, diamond, and platinum.
circa 1925.

L. 3 ⁷/₈″, L. 9.8cm.

A rounded rectangular evening comb carved from a single piece of tortoiseshell in a conforming tortoiseshell case. The hinged case is enhanced with a band of rose diamond set in platinum along the closure with a central clasp in rose diamond in an Oriental motif.

Fabricator: Cartier, London.

Cartier Stock Number: None.

Provenance: Auction: Christie's, London, April 29, 1987, #151, illustrated.
The Lindemann Collection, New York, from 1987.

Comments:

With emergence of the handbag as a primary costume accessory during the 1920s many cosmetic items were fashioned of costly materials. Single items, such as a comb, were frequently accompanied by a lipstick case, a compact, or a cigarette case.

Arbitrarily juxtaposed here against a *belle époque* ornament, this Art Deco haircomb points to many of the differences between the two styles. Although the many "garland" style objects, such as the above belt buckle and the bell push (catalogue number XVI) were functional, this aspect received heightened emphasis in Cartier Art Deco designs. Enamel continued to be employed by Art Deco designers. Only rarely used as a field, however, enamel was usually employed to delineate and enhance contrasting elements. Increasingly, the emphasis shifted from these metallic surfaces to natural elements, high-keyed colors, and textural contrasts. In this elegant haircomb this evolution is reflected in the use of warm, glowing tortoiseshell contrasted against the hard glitter of diamonds. Such combinations had frequently appeared in the Art Nouveau designs of his contemporaries, but were not prominent in Louis Cartier's work until the emergence of the Art Deco mode.

PLATE XX

FRAME

Enamel, silver, and silver-gilt.
circa 1909.

Diam. 7″
Diam. 17.8cm.

A circular silver frame in dark blue radiant *guilloché* enamel with opaque white enamel borders. The reverse is engine-turned silver-gilt with a gilt metal open work strut.

Fabricator: Bako Workshop, Paris,
           for Cartier, Paris.

Cartier Stock Number: #3052.

Provenance: Mme. Lyon.
           Obsidian, London.
           The Lindemann Collection, New York,
           from 1983.

Comments:

In contrast to those of the Second Empire, Edwardian interiors were generally decorated with dark wood furniture and made dimmer by heavy drapes that effectively blocked external light. To relieve the artificially created gloom of such environments, a wide assortment of bright *objets de vertu* were clustered around the rooms on tables and other flat surfaces. At this time, the photograph was still a novelty, and fashion dictated a number of framed photographs. Most of the leading jewelers of the day offered a wide variety of such frames. Cartier frequently employed the use of a white enamel band at the inner edge of the frame, which helped to set off the photograph. The Bako *atelier* supplied the House of Cartier with numerous highly finished enamelled objects. Many of these Bako objects were reminiscent of earlier Russian enamelled pieces.

The photograph is of George Lindemann, Jr. mounted on the French stallion *Sans Pardon* taken in 1986.

For further comments and comparison, see catalogue numbers XXVIII, XLI, and LI.

PLATE XXI

CIGAR HOLDER

Amber, enamel, and gold.
circa 1902-1909.

L. 3⁷/₈″
L. 9.8cm.

A short bulbous holder executed in amber. The design is enhanced with alternating bands of incised gold and opaque white enamel on the flute and similarly treated rondelle. An entwined script cipher, "DL", in white enamel on gold is applied to the flute.

Fabricator: Cartier, Paris.

Cartier Stock Number: None.

Provenance: Obsidian, London.
The Lindemann Collection, New York, from 1985.

Comments:

This holder reflects Edwardian taste prevalent at the turn of the century. It contrasts the lush hue and texture of amber with the simple white enamel bands, eschewing any stylized geometric ornament. This unusual holder is equipped with a unique telescoping facility for ejecting spent cigars.

It is accompanied by its original fitted red leather case.

CIGARETTE HOLDER

Nephrite, coral, diamond, ivory, and gold.
circa 1927.

L. 6″
L. 15.2cm

A long tapered holder with a nephrite funnel, a red coral tube, and carved ivory mouthpiece. The funnel is set in gold and enhanced with two rose diamond and coral palmettes. The coral tube is secured between two rondelles; one of *pavé*-set rose diamond, and one of gold.

Fabricator: Lavabre Workshop, Paris,
for Cartier, Paris.

Cartier Stock Number: #02432.

Provenance: Obsidian, London.
The Lindemann Collection, New York, from 1985.

Comments:

Prior to World War I smoking by both sexes was acceptable only in Tsarist Russia. With the general international acceptance of public smoking following the war, the cigarette holder became an implement of fashion for both men and women. As usual, Cartier was ready to supply its customers with elegant and stylish designs.

While the Edwardian taste favored muted color contrasts and curvilinear designs, the Art Deco mode dictated exactly the opposite. The simple and practical shape of the cigarette holder became elegantly stylized into a long tapered trumpet. This basic form is emphasized, rather than diffused, with concentric rondelles of glittering diamond and lustruous gold accenting the contrasting tones of the nephrite, coral, and ivory sections.

This piece is signed and numbered on the gold finial and is accompanied by its original fitted red leather case.

Similar holders are featured in *I Gioielle Degli Anni '20-40 Cartier e i Grandi del Deco*, Palazzo Fortuny, Venice, 1986, plate 53; *Retrospective Louis Cartier, Masterworks of Art Deco*, Los Angeles County Museum, 1982-1983, plates 53 and 54; and *Retrospective Louis Cartier, 101 Years of the Jeweler's Art*, Cartier, New York, 1976, plate 63.

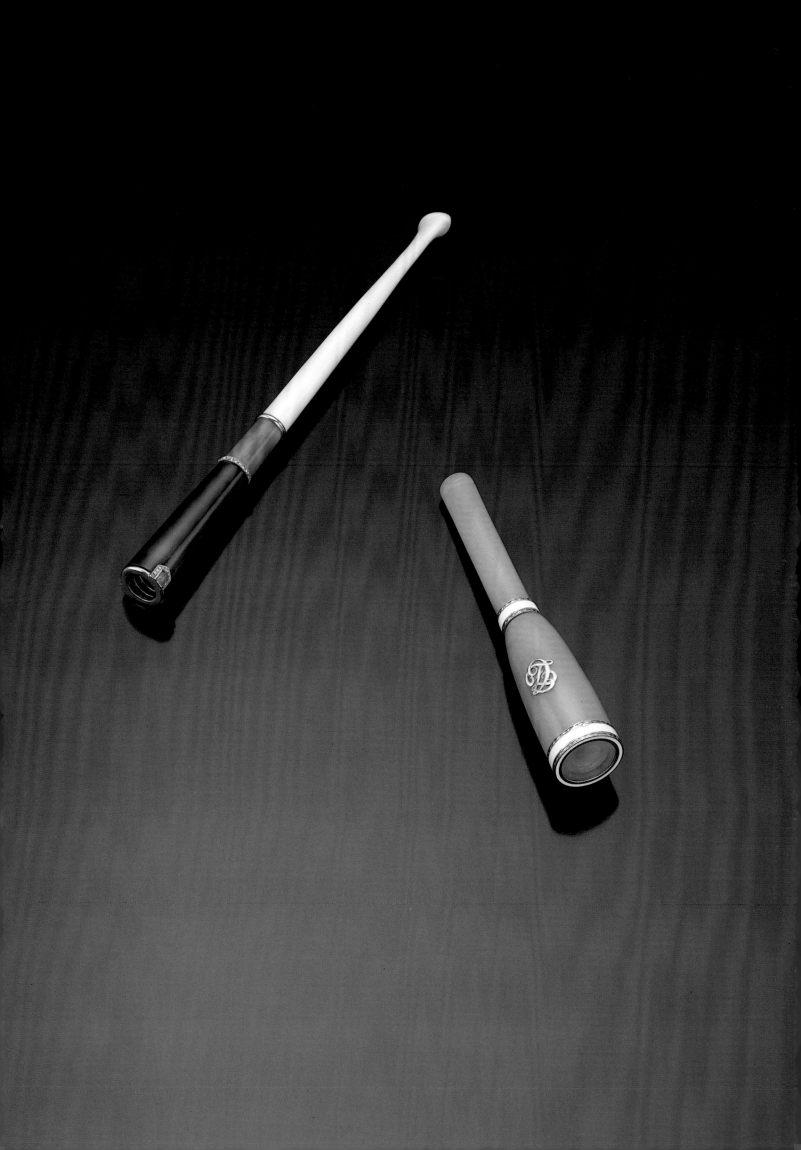

PLATE XXII

OPERA GLASSES

Diamond, horn, enamel, gold, and optical glass. 1911.

L. 3 ¼″ W. 4″
L. 8.2cm. W. 10.1cm.

Two trumpet-shaped glasses on a gold frame with carved horn rim and adjusting wheel. The glass cases and screw are transparent amber *guilloché* enamel. Royal blue enamel medallions centered with a rose diamond and suspended from a diamond tasselled bowknot in a *pavé*-set diamond garland adorn the side of each case. The frame is gold with edges of trellis-patterned white enamel. The rims and adjusting wheel are enhanced with ribbons of emerald enamel twining about *pavé*-set diamond rings with beaded gold. The front is embellished with blue enamel bands centered with a rose diamond and circumscribed by gold.

Fabricator: Lavabre Workshop, Paris,
    for Cartier, Paris.

Cartier Stock Number: #8398.

Provenance: Patrick Bonhenry, Paris.
    The Lindemann Collection, New York,
    from 1986.

Comments:

Opera glasses were a fashionable accessory from the 1870s and were regarded as a "finishing touch" to an elaborate evening *toilette*. Purely functional in intent, the glasses were raised to the level of decorative works of art by their embellishment with polychrome enamels and gemstones.

The tassellated and bowknot motifs are a revival of the Louis XVI (reigned 1774-1793) taste, which was well within the confines of Cartier's "garland" style. Certainly such glasses would have admirably complemented the diamond jewelry then regarded as the most suitable for appearances at the opera. The use of horn here, however, hints at the unorthodox combination of ordinary and precious materials which had so often marked Art Nouveau compositions. Although Cartier retailed some items in this style, it was not a personal favorite of Louis Cartier's and, hence, few completely Art Nouveau objects were created by Cartier workshops. A notable exception to this was Charpentier's *atelier* in rue de Richelieu which had earlier provided "winged" and "Renaissance" tiaras to the firm.

PLATE XXIII

LOVE BIRDS

Brown agate, diamond, bowenite, ivory, enamel,
and gold.
circa 1912.

Ht. 3¾"
Ht. 9.5cm.

Two stylized cockatoos, intricately carved in translucent brown agate with rose diamond eyes and gold legs and feet, rest on a short ivory perch. The base of the perch is decorated with a gold, white enamel and pink *guilloché* enamel band. The whole raised on a square bowenite base.

Fabricator: Cartier, Paris.

Cartier Stock Number: #44881.

Provenance: Obsidian, London.
The Lindemann Collection, New York,
from 1986.

Comments:

The image of two birds on a perch appeared in 1881 and later in the 1890s was adapted for use in a series of brooches. So popular was the "lovebird" motif that it became a Cartier tradition and continued to be reproduced in various forms well after the turn of the century. This diminutive sculpture is generally regarded as one of the most charming and engaging of the "lovebird" compositions.

Cartier preferred elegantly stylized images rather than a literal representation as would have earlier been the case with the hardstone animals and birds created by Peter Carl Fabergé (1846-1920). The inspiration for Cartier's sculptures, however, must certainly be credited to the Russian court jeweler. In 1904 Cartier began creating many such inspired pieces. This is partly explained by Cartier's growing Russian clientele, such as Grand Duke Paul and Princess Lobanov-Dolgorouky, who frequently visited or kept homes in the vicinity of Paris and expected to find objects similar to those in their homeland at fashionable Parisian shops. In addition, several events spurred the interest of western Europeans in Russian culture. At the 1867 World Fair, the 1878 Exposition, and again at the 1900 *Exposition Universelle*, Russian dignitaries and artisans had been selected for special honors. Then in 1909, the appearance of the *Ballets russes* in Paris revitalized this interest. The effect of these experiences with Russian art and culture on Cartier designs can not be undervalued. In many ways, they are linked to two of the major styles of Cartier. First, French craftsmen were reawakened to their own eighteenth-century heritage by the success of the early expositions; thus giving impetus to the creation of the "garland" style. Secondly, one of the major tenets of the Art Deco style, an emphasis on color contrasts, was directly inspired by the brilliant sets of the *Ballets russes*.

This sculpture is accompanied by an original fitted red leather case.

For further comments and comparison, see catalogue numbers XVIII and XXIV.

A similar bird sculpture is in the collection of the Musée Cartier, Geneva, Switzerland.

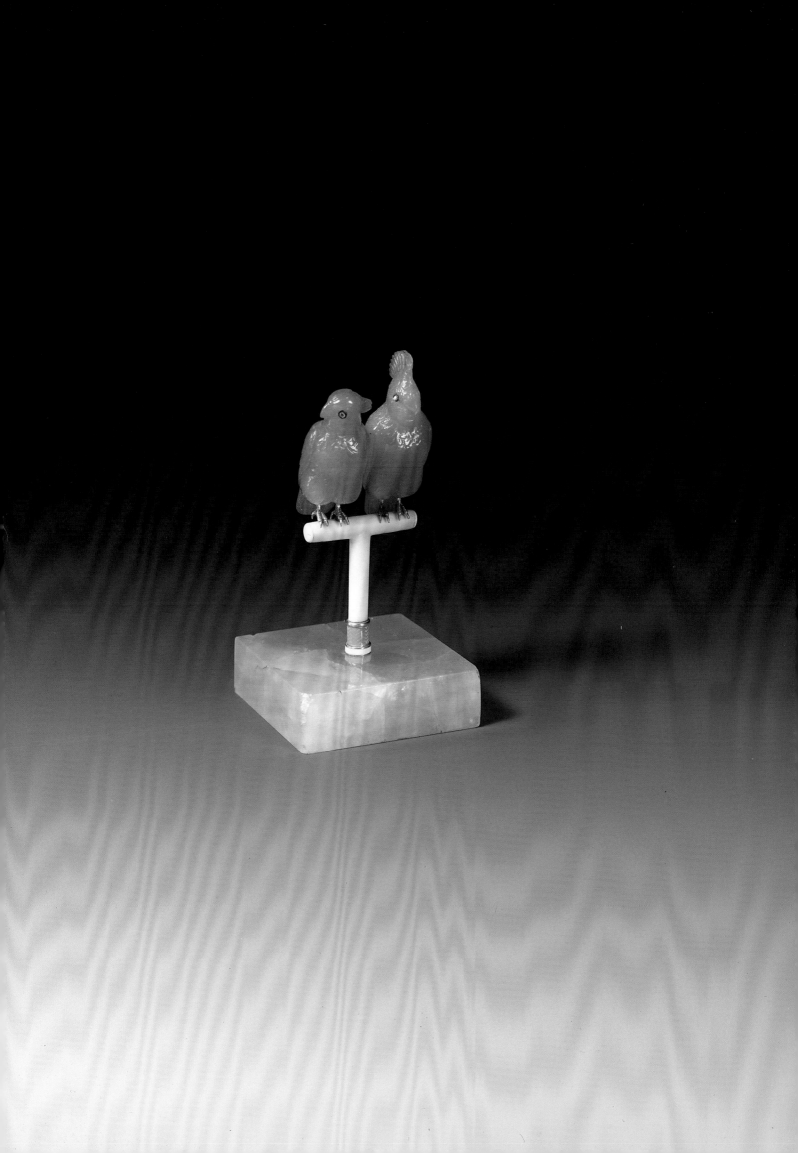

PLATE XXIV

HERON

Agate, jade, rock crystal, diamond, lapis-lazuli, and gold.
1924.

Ht. 4¼″ W. 3½″ D. 2½″
Ht. 10.8cm. W. 8.9cm. D. 6.3cm.

A carved translucent brown agate bird with rose diamond eyes and 18 karat gold legs and feet. The bird walks upon two carved jade lily pads enhanced with cabochon moonstone dewdrops. Three carved coral blossoms float on the rock crystal base carved to depict rippled water. A carved green jade frog with rose diamond eyes rests upon a lapis-lazuli boulder at the front edge of the base.

Fabricator: Coüet Workshop, Paris, for Cartier, Paris.

Cartier Stock Number: #039.

Provenance: Auction: Christie's, New York, March 5, 1985, #329, illustrated. The Lindemann Collection, New York, from 1985.

Comments:

The House of Cartier was one of the first western European jewelers to incorporate carved hardstone animals and birds into their repertoire of *objets de vertu*. As early as 1904, such miniature figurines which had been popularized by the Russian court jeweler Peter Carl Fabergé (1846-1920) appeared in Cartier's inventory. Unique to Cartier at first, as the Paris *ateliers* became proficient in their production, the market was soon saturated with imitations.

The commercial climate and his continued absorption of other influences prompted Louis Cartier to begin producing these charming landscapes-*cum*-animals in 1907. More elaborate in concept than the works of Fabergé, Cartier combined several elements accomplished from a wide variety of materials to create miniature total environments.

The manner in which a single moment in nature is captured indicates the Japanese inspiration of the piece. Here, the instant depicted is that just before the heron captures its prey. Characteristically, Cartier was more interested in a sumptuous, chic presentation than a literal translation. However, whether the image was of two birds in a blossomed cherry tree, a magnolia, or an insect, the charming aura of transitoriness pervades the work.

The heron is accompanied by a fitted red leather case.

For further comments and comparison, see catalogue numbers XVIII and XXIII.

For a similar bird sculpture see, *The H. Robert Greene Collection of Art Deco*, Christie's, Geneva, November 16, 1978, plate 513.

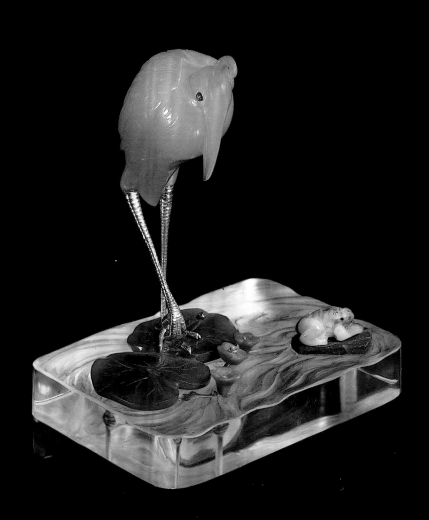

PLATE XXV

SINGLE CIGAR CASE

Grey agate, sapphire, diamond, enamel, and
gold.
circa 1924.

Ht. 1″ W. 7/8″ L. 7 1/2″
Ht. 2.5cm. W. 2.2cm. L. 19cm.

A narrow elongated rectangular container of carved
grey agate. The sides are decorated with a broad
band of gold enhanced with a circle and dot pattern
in white and dark blue *guilloché* enamel. The
clasps are elegantly appointed gold collet cabochon
sapphires. The top of the case is centered by a rose
diamond-encrusted gold imperial Romanov crest.

Fabricator: Cartier, Paris.

Cartier Stock Number: None.

Provenance: The Lindemann Collection, New York,
from 1985.

Comments:

This case embodies the essence of Art Deco
taste; its sleek luxurious design and practical use
mark it as a product of an aesthetic determined by
function. Cartier's inventory traditionally included
a variety of such items. The increased emphasis on
usefulness after World War I reflects the changing
public attitude and heralds the Art Deco mode.

This case may have been supplied to Cartier by
the workshop of Aristide Fourrier (1875-1941), suc-
cessor to the Berquin-Varangoz firm, which had
supplied the early flower pieces. Fourrier was adamant in recognizing his artistic debt to Peter Carl
Fabergé (1846-1920) and referred to him consistently as his mentor.

Considering the provenance of this piece, its leg-
acy from the work of Fabergé is appropriate. Cartier's dealings with the Russian aristocracy date to
1860 when Prince Saltikov purchased an emerald
bracelet from the boulevard des Italiens shop. The

relationship between the firm and members of the
Tsarist court grew and eventually led to the estab-
lishment of a Cartier branch at 28 Quai de la Cour
in St. Petersburg, December 1908. Overcoming the
sometimes vindictive and underhanded competition and the inherent Russian reticence to change
suppliers, Cartier's attracted many notable aristocrats including Princess Zenaïde Youssoupov
whose jewel cases were of legendary fame, Grand
Duchess Xenia, and Cartier's avid supporter Grand
Duchess Vladimir. Through Grand Duchess Xenia's mother, the widowed Empress Marie Feodo-
rovna, Cartier even received an audience at
Tsarskoe Selo with Tsar Nicholas II and his wife,
Tsarina Alexandra. The relationships established
at this time lasted for many years. As the date of
this piece suggests, even after the Revolution Cartier retained close affiliations with the Romanov
family.

PLATE XXVI

VASE

White agate, enamel, gold, and rock crystal.
circa 1925.

Ht. 3⁷/₈″ W. 2 ³/₈″ D. 2 ³/₈″
Ht. 9.8cm. W. 6cm. D. 6cm.

A square vase set upon a carved coved and footed white agate base with a rock crystal lining. The four sides are violet sunray *guilloché* enamel with white enamel borders. An enamelled white medallion with a swirling leaf pattern in turquoise and yellow enamel enhances the center of each side. The rim of the vase is gold chased in a trellis pattern.

Fabricator: Bako Workshop, Paris, for Cartier, Paris.

Cartier Stock Number: #2107.

Provenance: Auction: Sotheby's, St. Moritz, February 20-22, 1986, #514, illustrated.
The Lindemann Collection, New York, from 1986.

Comments:

This vase represents a remarkable synthesis in the transition between the "garland" and Art Deco styles. In this instance, the *guilloché* enamel fields, medallions, and opaque white borders commonly associated with the "garland" style have been handled with a keen interest in the tenets of the Art Deco mode. The severe geometric outline of this elegant vase functions well against the lush violet *guilloché* enamelled fields and simplified medallions of each side. Absent are the characteristic bowknots and tassels of the "garland" style, and the Cartier standard white borders are here used to heighten and delineate the contrasts of the planes. Such contrasts were characteristic of the Art Deco style as interpreted by the House of Cartier.

It is thought that this vase was executed by the Bako *atelier*, Paris, on order from Cartier. It bears French gold marks and is accompanied by a fitted red leather case stamped "Cartier."

PLATE XXVII

VANITY

Seed pearl, sapphire, enamel, gold, and mirror.
circa 1925.

Ht. 1 ⁷/₈" L. 3 ⁷/₈" D. 1"
Ht. 4.8cm. L. 9.8cm. D. 2.5cm.

A compressed cylindrical 18 karat gold case decorated with fine stripes of pale blue *guilloché* enamel. The ends of the case are enhanced with
polished gold and dark blue arabesque borders,
and studded with lines of seed pearls. The thumbpiece is set with three cabochon sapphires. The interior is fitted with a mirror, a pill box, a lipstick
holder, two powder compartments with hinged covers, and a cigarette compartment.

Fabricator: Lavabre Workshop, Paris, for Cartier,
Paris.

Cartier Stock Number: #0373.

Provenance: Auction: Christie's, New York,
April 24, 1985, #49, illustrated.
The Lindemann Collection, New York,
from 1985.

Comments:

As the forerunner of the handbag, the multi-
function vanity, or *nécessaire*, was aptly suited to
Art Deco taste. It was both practical and decorative. Fitted with several compartments, the vanity
provided storage for an assortment of items. During
the heyday of the vanity in the 1920s and '30s, it
was no longer surprising for women to smoke in
public and cosmetics had come into general vogue.
Cartier's designed a variety of these cases which
stylishly included compartments for powder containers, pill boxes, cigarettes and lipsticks.

Simultaneously, the vanity case was the perfect
palette for Cartier's Art Deco designs. Made of
sturdy materials such as precious metals or lacquered woods, they were relatively variable in
shape and were easily applied with enamels and
gems in a wide range of motifs. Although it lacks
the bold color contrasts associated with the style,
the Art Deco date of this vanity is belied by its
sleek geometric profile and the stylized Islamic-in-
spired arabesque adornment.

The Henri Lavabre *atelier* in the rue Ticque-
tonne, Paris, was a major supplier to Cartier of
gemset enamelled objects as well as such articles
as "winged" neoclassical tiaras (1909).

For further comments and comparison, see catalogue numbers XLV, and L.

PLATE XXVIII

FRAME

Diamond, onyx, coral, and gold.
circa 1925.

Ht. 5 ½″ W. 4″
Ht. 14cm. W. 10.2cm.

An upright rectangular miniature frame of carved black onyx, the wide onyx border accented by a narrow interior band of gold channel-set red coral batons. This band is broken at the centers of each side by sections of *páve*-set rose diamonds mounted in platinum. The frame is further enhanced in each corner with fleurettes of *páve*-set rose diamonds in platinum with red coral gold collet centers. A gold lattice-work strut is attached to the back.

Fabricator: Cartier, New York.

Cartier Stock Number: None.

Provenance: Obsidian, London.
The Lindemann Collection, New York, from 1984.

Comments:

Louis Cartier had early advocated the production of useful objects. In fact, such items were well within the Cartier range long before his directive preceding the 1925 *Exposition Internationale des Arts décoratifs et industriels modernes*: "We must make it our business to build up an inventory that responds to the moral mood of the public by producing articles which have a useful function but which are also decorated in the Cartier style" (Nadelhoffer, H., *Cartier: Jewelers Extraordinary*, Harry N. Abrams, New York, 1984, p. 197). Photograph frames, which had become fashionable during the Edwardian epoch at the turn of the century and remained in vogue throughout the 1920s and '30s, were excellent subjects for the application of this "functional jewel" concept.

Intended to complement and harmonize with the fashionable geometrically stylized interiors of the day, jeweled frames such as this are a perfect example of the Art Deco synthesis between the decorative arts and architecture. Such high-style Art Deco frames were a specialty of the House of Cartier. Following the preference of Louis Cartier for dramatic contrasts of material and color, the fabricator of this frame has juxtaposed the softly glistening surfaces of onyx and coral with gold and the hard glitter of diamonds. The use of boldly contrasting hues had come into vogue as a result of the work of the *Fauve* painters, who had their first Paris exhibition in 1905, and the influence of the *Ballets russes* whose vividly colored stage sets had taken Paris by storm in 1909.

The frame is accompanied by its original fitted red leather case.

The photograph is of Mrs. Lindemann taken in 1941 in Florida.

For further comments and comparison, see catalogue numbers XX, XLI, and LI.

PLATE XXIX

GENTLEMAN'S DRESSING SET

Coral, enamel, silver, and mirror.
circa 1925.

Mirror Ht: 14 ¹/₂", Ht. 37cm.
Timepiece Ht: 6 ¹¹/₁₆", Ht. 17cm.

A fifteen piece set with a standing looking glass, one hand mirror, a pair of large square bottles and a smaller pair, a pair of clothes brushes, a rectangular casket and tray, a pair of dodecagonal boxes and a clock. Each piece is mounted with facet cut mirrored panels in a trellis pattern within a black enamel cagework, enhanced with bands of red coral set in gold, and the crowned cypher of His Highness the Maharajah Sir Bhudindra Singh.

Fabricator: Cartier, Paris.

Cartier Stock Number: Timepiece: #2432.

Provenance: The Private Collection of H.H. the Maharajah Sir Bhudindra Singh of Patiala, the Moti Bash Palace, Patiala. The Heirs of H.H. the Maharajah Sir Bhudindra Singh. Obsidian, London. The Lindemann Collection, New York, from 1988.

Comments:

In 1925, H.H. the Maharajah Sir Bhudindra Singh of Patiala (1891-1938), handed over to Cartier the most valuable pieces from his treasury, including the Victoria or De Beers diamond, for remodelling. The public exhibition of them held by Cartier when they were completed three years later attracted such notables as J. P. Morgan, the Duchess of Alba, and Mrs. Laura Corrigan and caused a veritable sensation. The Maharajah was one of Cartier's favorite and most flamboyant clients. His Moti Bash Palace covered eleven acres, was staffed by thirty-five hundred retainers, and had a stable of five hundred horses for his personal use. His attire was commensurate. When in native dress, his ample form was girded with multiple ropes of pearls, diamonds, and emeralds. For an excellent photograph of the Maharajah of Patiala in ceremonial dress with jewels by Cartier, see Gautier, G., *Cartier, The Legend*, Arlington Books, London, 1983, page 189.

Dressing sets which had been a Cartier standard since the 1860s, became popular items in the 1920s and '30s. Executed in a variety of materials, they were especially favored by Cartier's wealthy Indian clients. Besides the Maharajah of Patiala, the Maharanee of Nawanagar owned an exquisite set made of Chinese lacquer and obsidian. This set, however, fabricated in diamond-shaped faceted mirror is indicative of a whole range of Cartier creations. With the severe geometrical emphasis placed on their design, the objects in this range presage the Art Moderne style of the 1940s.

PLATE XXX

ASHTRAY

Jade, coral, enamel, and gold.
circa 1925-1930.

Ht. 2 ⅞″ W. 5 ⅝″ D. 2 ¾″
Ht. 7.3cm. W. 14.3cm. D. 7cm.

An elongated oval tray of carved green jade with a cigarette rest on either end. It is enhanced with four melon-ribbed red coral bosses set with platinum collet rose diamonds. The center supports a rectangular reeded gold match box holder decorated with black enamel borders and similar ribbed red coral and diamond bosses.

Fabricator: Cartier, New York.

Cartier Stock Number: None.

Provenance: Auction: Christie's, New York, April 15, 1986, #29, illustrated.
The Lindemann Collection, New York, from 1986.

Comments:

Cartier had been designing smokers' requisites since the turn of the century. With the advent of the Art Deco mode, ashtrays, lighters, match boxes, and cigarette cases were ideal subjects for the application of the popular dual function concept. The use of ribbed diamond-centered coral bosses and stylized black enamel borders imparts an air of Moghul opulence and style to this ashtray.

This ashtray is accompanied by a fitted red leather case.

PEN

Agate, coral, enamel, and gold.
circa 1925-1930.

L. 6 ⅛″, L. 15.5 cm.

A long round cartridge of carved agate with coral rondelles. The cartridge is enhanced with a gold collet coral cabochon end. The tip holder is 18 karat gold with geometric black enamel bands at either end.

Fabricator: Cartier, London.

Cartier Stock Number: #5817.

Provenance: Auction: Christie's, London, April 29, 1987, #142, illustrated.
The Lindemann Collection, New York, from 1987.

Comments:

In keeping with Louis Cartier's concept of the "functional jewel", the Art Deco treatment was employed on a wide variety of objects. Like the ashtray, writing implements were perfect symbols of this aesthetic. Often created as parts of complete desks sets, as in the *Ecran* Mystery clock/Standish (catalogue number LXIII), Cartier produced a number of mechanical pencils and pens. While some were accomplished in simple combinations of materials, others such as this one display the full range of Art Deco taste. In this case, the sleek form of a pen in translucent agate with bright coral and gold accents fully integrates the Art Deco penchant for function and contrasting colors.

THE FLOWERS

The House of Cartier early numbered a select group of Russians among its clientele; in 1860, Prince Saltikov purchased an enamelled emerald bracelet. As the fame and prestige of the House spread, the number of Russian patrons increased and widened to. include members of the imperial family. Interwoven with this phenomenon was the fact that Russian art since Tsar Peter the Great (reigned 1689-1725), and Empress Catherine II (reigned 1762-1796) had been fundamentally indebted to France. Thus, Russians frequenting Cartier's premises were doubly susceptible to the French aura exuded by its objects. Under Napoléon III's glittering Second Empire (1852-1871), France had been notably receptive to Russian artists at the influential Paris expositions of 1867 and 1878. A series of coveted gold and silver medals was awarded to Russian goldsmiths. This cordial atmosphere had brought a number of wealthy Russians to Paris, and this colony was augmented following the assassination of Alexander III in 1881 when many feared insurrection in Russia and established themselves in the French capital. These *émigrés*, who easily moved in the highest Parisian circles, unwittingly created a vogue for Russian objects. This transplanted taste included enamelled objects, hardstone figures and floral groups. Given these influences, it is not suprising that Cartier fell under the spell of the Russian court jeweler Peter Carl Fabergé (1846-1920) who by 1900 was producing an extraordinary range of *objets de vertu* and a rich series of enamels generally accepted as the world's finest.

Since both Alfred and Louis Cartier were astute businessmen and devoted to the success of the family firm, it followed that they would attempt to rival Russian goods and, in some instances, to import them for sale in Paris.[1] In one area, the influence of Fabergé fell upon particularly fertile ground, and this was the rare flowers and floral groups that Cartier produced in response to the celebrated Fabergé prototypes. In spite of an instan-

taneous acceptance, the flowers remain among the most rare of all Cartier productions. The Lindemann Collection is noteworthy for its present inclusion of five of these unusual masterworks and a sixth related although very different example, a pair of potted cacti executed in an archetypal Art Deco manner.

In the production of exquisitely wrought artificial flowers, both Fabergé and Cartier were responding to a European tradition which was rooted in Renaissance art. The numerous courts of Middle Europe had a tradition of gold and gem-set floral pieces. The Habsburg Dynasty of Austria commissioned a series of gemstone bouquets during the seventeenth century.[2] The great eighteenth-century Empress, Maria-Theresa (reigned 1745-1780), mother of the ill-fated Marie-Antoinette (reigned 1774-1793), followed this tradition with the order of a jeweled bouquet from the jeweler Grosser.[3] The Electors of Saxony had also ordered gem-set floral groups set in vases. In Russia, similar eighteenth-century compositions in precious metals and gems are still seen in the collections of the Hermitage and the Kremlin Armoury Museum. It is thought likely that Fabergé actually was familiar with these antique specimens. During the late nineteenth and early twentieth centuries, Chinese glassworkers had been producing elaborately wrought blossoms in glass for ornamental arrangements. These were usually composed of hundreds of individually crafted petals assembled into such large blooms as chrysanthemums. These realistic artifices were viewed enthusiastically by Westerners at the great international expositions of the era. It is possible that both Cartier and Fabergé were also familiar with these *tour-de-force* examples of the Oriental glassmaker's art. Certainly some of the 1920s flowers of Cartier were to use a similar technique. Whatever the specific inspiration, it may safely be stated that flowers composed of precious materials were part of the history of stylish aristocratic European taste and that both Fabergé and Cartier responded to this established tradition.

Cartier and Fabergé shared the concept that the flowers be reproduced in materials which would most effectively lend themselves to a final effect. Neither was interested in the use of stones simply for their intrinsic value. The ornamental floral group could, in fact, be made of any material as long as its design, decorative qualities and workmanship remained paramount. The fact that such combinations were often unorthodox was of no significance to either man. Thus, cabochons suited the tastes of both creators, for their softly radiant surfaces did not distract the eye from the overall design in the way a coruscating faceted gem would. It is interesting to note that both men knew and collected Japanese art; this was to have a pronounced effect on the production of their flowers although each man's reaction to and interpretation of that art was completely different.

The floral groups by Fabergé, whose production had begun in the late years of the last quarter of the nineteenth century, concentrated primarily upon reproducing the natural appearance of the specific plant as closely as possible in the selected gems and hardstones. So successful was Fabergé in his choice of materials and in the exactitude of his workmanship that contemporary critics denigrated his floral pieces as too realistic. In general, the Fabergé flowers were of small scale, usually no more than five inches in height. Most commonly, these botanically correct compositions were placed in clear rock crystal vases carved to appear as if they contained water. Occasionally, the limpid rock crystal vase was exchanged for a flowerpot formed of jasper or agate. In the floral groups destined for the Russian imperial family, Fabergé sometimes designed more elaborate vases, often enhanced with the brilliant enamels for which his firm was renowned. The salient feature, however, of all the Fabergé floral creations was that they were intended to stand independently upon a table, desk or mantelshelf. Such a placement enhanced the illusion of their floral reality and, in the case of owners residing in Russia, reminded one pleasantly of the end of the long, enveloping winter.

While there is little doubt that Cartier flower pieces were initially inspired by those of Fabergé, their final form and interpretation could not be more different. The Cartier flowers are invariably of a larger scale than Fabergé's, and are customarily placed within rectangular glass vitrines. These vitrines, or cases, are often ornamented at the upper corners with bronze spandrels of Chinese inspiration. The result of this architectonic encasing is that Cartier flowers appear to exist in the independent environment of a miniature hothouse. Using these vitrines as an integral part of the design, Cartier had the distinct advantage of being released from demanding verisimilitude. Within the decorative "greenhouses", Cartier was free to concentrate upon more stylized arrangements of the flowers simply because of the autonomous environment. The vitrines isolated the compositions from their immediate surroundings; therefore, the contents are not absorbed into the general ambience of a room as tends to be the case with Fabergé's freestanding flowers. Cartier's knowledge of traditional Japanese *ikebana*, or flower arranging, was useful here, for it permitted to depict more effectively such natural phenomena as broken stems or to create arbitrary, aesthetically pleasing arrangements. The *ikebana* influence is also to be detected in the Japanese-style platforms on which Cartier frequently placed his floral compositions; these and the containers they supported are occasionally sprinkled with cabochon moonstone dewdrops, thus suggesting an early morning hour.

While the floral works of Fabergé and Cartier occasionally overlapped, the two houses were essentially interested in different types of flowers.[4] Fabergé's intense concern with realism drew him naturally to smaller specimens such as cornflowers, mistletoe sprays, lilies-of-the-valley, buttercups, and orange blossoms while larger more showy blossoms; hydrangeas, magnolias, irises, certain types of lilies and tulips were frequently encountered in the Cartier productions. Cartier probably preferred these subjects precisely because they adapted well to a presentation which imparted the "impression" of the living flower accompanied by a simultaneously chic and elegant appearance. These effects were created by subtle stylizations of the plant form; at no point did Cartier feel constrained by a need for exact naturalism. At the height of the Art Deco style, he further stylized the leaves and calyxes of his standard flowers in order to adhere more closely to the dictates of the new international style.

Further differentiating the productions of the two houses is Cartier's utilization of a greater range of materials for the containers and stands of his floral compositions. While Fabergé generally employed rock crystal or jasper, Cartier explored a wider range of colored agates and lapis-lazuli as well as rock crystal and jasper. The Cartier shapes were distinctive from the diminutive rock crystal vases and jasper flowerpots of Fabergé. The Cartier planters and tubs were often further embellished with cabochons of sapphire and other colored stones at the stiles and corners; other flower containers by the firm were enhanced with gold mounts simulating wrought-iron forms and were sparked with small diamond "nailheads." Frequently, the hardstones from which the containers were constructed were painstakingly selected to match the flower growing in them.[5] This concept differed dramatically from that of Fabergé, the materials of whose vessels were very different from the blooms they contained and were intended to set off the flowers dramatically.

Cartier's flowers were initially commissioned from the Berquin-Varangoz workshop, a hardstone specialty house operated by the widow of the founder at Saint-Siméon in Seine-et-Marne. Madame Berquin-Varangoz was bought out by Aristide Fourrier (1875-1941) in 1918, and the shop name was changed to reflect the new ownership. In spite of the already noted differences between the flowers Berquin-Varangoz/Fourrier supplied Cartier and those of Fabergé, Fourrier maintained throughout his career that Fabergé was his inspiration and mentor. Be that as it may, the methods by which the Cartier flower pieces were produced differed markedly from those of the House of Fabergé. Both Berquin-Varangoz *veuve* and later, Fourrier, composed a copper model of the desired flower and sent this to Paris for approval or modification. Once final approval was secured, the piece was executed in enamelled or oxidized silver, with the flowerheads fabricated in glass, hardstone or enamels. The leaves were either also enamelled or carved of jade or aventurine quartz. The practice of forming stems and, occasionally, leaves and calyxes of enamelled or oxidized silver differed markedly from that of Fabergé, who invariably used cast, drawn and chased gold for these purposes.

The Lindemann Collection is remarkable in its possession of a superb pair of jade cacti in chalcedony bowls (catalogue number XXVI). The bold sculptural stylizations of these elegant plant interpretations serve as an effective counterpoint to the somewhat less robust, more lyrical florals. Louis Cartier's personal preference for the sleek stylizations of the Art Deco manner is well-known, and these small-scale but visually arresting pieces stand as testimony to the skill of the Cartier designers and fabricators. One of two pairs presently known, the cacti make, perhaps, the most bold visual statement about Cartier's 1926 remove from the initial end of the century inspiration of Fabergé. Although these models were not designed to stand in the usual Cartier-designed vitrines and are therefore more akin to Fabergé's freestanding floral pieces, their dazzling color contrasts and candid abstraction mark them as Art Deco objects of the highest style. As such, they stand at a considerable distance from the Edwardian floral elegancies of Fabergé and are but marginally related to Cartier's more common, but still rare, flower compositions.

In spite of their patent differences in conception, style and use of materials, the flower pieces of both Houses convey a sense of freshness and originality to the beholder. While many contend that Fabergé's flowers represent the zenith of his achievement, there can be little argument that the clocks of Cartier are his ultimate masterpieces. However, there is general agreement among scholars, collectors and curators that the flower compositions are the rarest creations of either maker. This is certainly substantiated in the case of Cartier by the infrequency with which one encounters his flowers reproduced in the standard reference books or leading periodicals.

[1] In his brilliant book, *Cartier: Jewelers Extraordinary* (Harry N . Abrams, New York, 1984, pp. 91-124.) the late Hans Nadelhoffer admirably explicated the influence of the aristocratic Russian taste, Russian art and, specifically, of Peter Carl Fabergé upon the creations of the House of Cartier.

[2] These are now preserved in the Kunsthistorisches Museum, Vienna.

[3] This bouquet may today be seen in the Schatzkammer of the Hofburg Palace, Vienna.

[4] Both firms, for example, produced a Morning Glory (see catalogue number XXXV for a Cartier example). However, Fabergé's eight and one-half inch example depicted a single polychrome-enamelled blossom twining about a silver pole while the Lindemann Collection example displays multiple blooms and grows around an ivory stake (see the exhibition catalogue *Fabergé, a Loan Exhibition for the Benefit of the Cooper-Hewitt Museum*, A la Vieille Russie, New York, April 22-May 21, 1983, page 126 number 469 and page 128, number 469). Fabergé also produced for Queen Alexandra of England a Japanese pine in red gold set with diamonds and growing in a bowenite vase set upon an aventurine quartz Japanese-style platform. The asymmetry of the pine's branches is akin to Cartier's *ikebana*-like compositions. However, this Fabergé model stands only five and one-eighth inches in height (see Snowman, A.K., *Carl Fabergé, Goldsmith to the Imperial Court of Russia*, Greenwich House/Crown Publishers, New York, 1983, page 86, lower center).

[5] See Nadelhoffer, H., *Cartier: Jewelers Extraordinary*, Harry N. Abrams, Inc., New York, 1984, color plate 1 for a pink opaline glass hydrangea planted in a gold and diamond-mounted pink agate footed tub).

PLATE XXXI

HYACINTH

Opaline quartz, aventurine quartz, and silver.
circa 1925.

Ht. 6 $^{11}/_{16}$"
Ht. 17cm.

Trumpeted carved violet colored opaline quartz blossoms are densely secured to an oxidized silver stem. The flower stalk rises from a quartz bulb between two carved aventurine quartz leaves. The potted plant sets on a white opaline quartz base, attached to a wood plinth, and covered with a glass vitrine.

Fabricator: Probably Fourrier Workshop, Saint-Siméon, Seine-et-Marne, for Cartier, Paris.

Cartier Stock Number: None.

Provenance: Obsidian, London.
The Lindemann Collection, New York, from 1985.

Comments:

Between 1905 and 1930 Cartier *ateliers* produced a variety of hardstone and enamel plants and flowers. Inspired by the earlier works of Peter Carl Fabergé (1846-1920), the character of Cartier's creations is subtly different.

Even in the earliest examples, these floral pieces exhibited affinities that presage the Art Deco style. From the beginning, Louis Cartier expressed an interest in combining contrasting materials into architectonic units, rather than mimicking the independent naturalistic flowers of Fabergé. He preferred elaborate, luxurious, and chic presentations typically placed in greenhouse-like glass vitrines that created a total environment in which the plants "live". Already simplified, the original format of their designs did not change much over the years. Only in the 1920s and '30s were they nominally modified to reflect the current taste for stylization.

Cartier's interests are vividly displayed in this sculpture of a hyacinth. A symbol of unconditional love and contentment, the hyacinth bloom dies at the height of its color as well as the foliage which has nurtured it, only to return with renewed beauty the following spring. Here, it is captured in glistening splendor at the pinnacle of its cycle; the lavender openwork cone contrasted against the glow of the aventurine leaves and the shining white symbol of its recurring nature. Although unusual for Cartier, the simple vitrine used here is an apt expression for the purity of the enclosed symbol; the more usual vitrine treatment featured bronze lambrequin-like corners inspired by Chinese motifs.

For further comments on Cartier's plant and flower sculptures, see catalogue numbers XXXII, XXXIII, XXXIV, XXXV, and XXXVI.

For similar pieces see, "Les Must de Cartier 1925", *Connaissance Des Arts*, April 1974; Nadelhoffer, H., *Cartier: Jewelers Extraordinary*, Thames and Hudson, 1984; color plate I. In *Cartier: The Cartier Room*, Grosvenor House Antiques Fair, London, 1986, a wisteria and a geranium plant, similar to the above, were exhibited.

PLATE XXXII

LILY

Opaline quartz, aventurine quartz, enamel, and silver.
circa 1925.

Ht. 7 $^{11}/_{16}$″
Ht. 19.5cm.

Enamelled pale blue blossoms on green enamelled stems grow from a pale jade pot of opaline quartz earth. The pot rests on a rose quartz stand set upon an ivory base. The whole is contained within a bronze mounted, glass vitrine on a wooden plinth.

Fabricator: Probably Fourrier Workshop,
Saint-Siméon, Seine-et-Marne,
for Cartier, Paris.

Cartier Stock Number: None.

Provenance: Auction: Christie's, Geneva, May 14, 1987, #408, illustrated.
The Lindemann Collection, New York, from 1987.

Comments:

Between 1905 and 1930 Cartier *ateliers* produced a variety of plant and flower sculptures. Although their basic style did not change much, during the Art Deco period they became more stylized to appeal to the taste of the period. A number of the Art Deco floral pieces display influences of non-European art similar to those being integrated into Cartier's concurrent designs for jewelry and other *objets de vertu*. Both Oriental and Near Eastern elements were absorbed into floral designs; however, Japanese and Chinese themes, like those seen in this sculpture, are the most prevalent.

In this example of a lily plant the Chinese influences are evident in the characteristic bronze lambrequin-like corners of the vitrine which have been engraved at the edge to suggest the traditional Chinese cloud motif. By so doing Cartier incorporates the Chinese concept of a total environment contained within an individual work of art. The Chinese aspects are enhanced by the *kang*-like stand on which the plant and its container rests.

By featuring a broken stem, the plant itself reflects the principles of formal Japanese flower arranging, *ikebana*. Noted for their deliberate inclusion of a flaw, *ikebana* arrangements often aspire to recreate a transitory moment. In this instance the moment has been captured just after the stem of the plant has snapped under the weight of the mature flower and just before the flower dies. By showing the blossom here in a less than perfect state, Cartier may have intended a witty ironic statement about the nature of human character of which the lily is an allegorical symbol.

For further comments on Cartier's plant and flower sculptures, see catologue numbers XXXI, XXXIII, XXXIV, XXXV, and XXXVI.

Similar flower pieces are illustrated in: "Les Must de Cartier 1925," *Connaissance Des Arts*, April 1974; and Nadelhoffer, H., *Cartier: Jewelers Extraordinary*, Thames and Hudson, 1984, color plate I. In *Cartier: The Cartier Room*, Grosvenor House Antiques Fair, London, 1986, a wisteria and a geranium plant, similar to the above, were exhibited.

PLATE XXXIII

CARNATION

Diamond, moonstone, aventurine quartz, agate, ivory, enamel, and silver.
circa 1925.

Ht. 5½"
Ht. 14 cm.

Three delicate pink-enamelled flowerheads with moonstone and rose diamond pistils rise from aventurine quartz leaves. The plant is in an agate pot, set on an agate stand, the whole is mounted on an ivory base.

Fabricator: Probably Fourrier Workshop,
Saint-Siméon, Seine-et-Marne,
for Cartier, Paris.

Cartier Stock Number: None.

Provenance: Auction: Christie's, Geneva, May 14, 1987, #407, illustrated.
The Lindemann Collection, New York, from 1987.

Comments:

This sculpture of a pink, a common variety carnation, exhibits many of the same Oriental influences as the lily (catalogue number XXXII). Similar Chinese and Japanese themes are present in the treatment of the stepped bronze corners on the vitrine, the *ikebana*-inspired floral arrangement, and the creation of a total and self-contained environment.

In contrast to the lily, however, the design of the pink is more stylized. Although the charm of transitoriness is captured, an ideal representation of nature, rather than an imperfection has been rendered. The pink is at the pinnacle of its splendor. Three perfect pink blossoms are contrasted against three dark green stalks of equal height and stature springing from a container of simple flower pot shape. Focus on the plant is intensified by its col-

orful juxtaposition against the subtle hues of the pot and ivory base.

Louis Cartier adeptly combined elements from a number of sources into the design for a single object. Although unverifiable, the decorative potential of these elements appear to be only one facet of their character. Louis Cartier was undoubtedly aware of their frequent symbolic associations. In this case, the pink is also a traditional symbol of marriage derived from a Flemish custom. The focus drawn to the plant itself by its idealized treatment and carefully orchestrated contrast to its surroundings may have been intended to emphasize its symbolic meaning, and would make it the perfect wedding or anniversary presentation.

For further comments on Cartier's plant and flower sculptures, see catalogue numbers XXXII, XXXIII, XXXIV, XXXV, and XXXVI.

For similar pieces see, "Les Must de Cartier 1925," *Connaissance Des Arts*, April 1974; Nadelhoffer, H., *Cartier: Jewelers Extraordinary*, Thames and Hudson, 1984, color plate I. In *Cartier: The Cartier Room*, Grosvenor House Antiques Fair, London, 1986, a wisteria and a geranium plant, similar to the above, were exhibited.

PLATE XXXIV

LILY-OF-THE-VALLEY

Opaline quartz, aventurine quartz, red jasper,
ivory, enamel, and gold.
circa 1925.

Ht. 7½"
Ht . 19cm.

Delicate bell-shaped carved colored opaline quartz
blossoms are suspended from green enamelled gold
stems. The two stems of flowers are flanked by
carved aventurine quartz leaves and set in a red jasper pot, the whole is raised on an ivory plinth set
on an ivory floor.

Fabricator: Probably Fourrier Workshop,
Saint-Siméon, Seine-et-Marne,
for Cartier, Paris.

Cartier Stock Number: None.

Provenance: Obsidian, London.
The Lindemann Collection, New York,
from 1985.

Comments:

A traditional symbol of renewal and purity, the
lily-of-the-valley as rendered here reflects the Oriental influences and Art Deco principles popular in
Cartier's designs of the 1920s and '30s. The
stepped bronze corners of the vitrine and elegantly
simplified floral arrangement recall the Chinese
and Japanese themes apparent in the lily (catalogue
number XXXII) and the carnation (catalogue number XXXIII). Although the basic types had
changed little in the preceding years, during the
1920s Cartier modified the designs to appeal to the
tastes then current. The Art Deco influence on the
design of the lily-of-the-valley is evident in the stylized treatment of the dainty bell-shaped blossoms
contrasted against the rich luster of the simplified
leaves and cubic ivory plinth on which the plant and
its pot rest.

For further comments on Cartier's plant and
flower sculptures, see catalogue numbers XXXI,
XXXII, XXXIII, XXXV, and XXXVI.

For similar pieces see, "Les Must de Cartier
1925," *Connaissance Des Arts*, April 1974; and Nadelhoffer, H., *Cartier: Jewelers Extraordinary*,
Thames and Hudson, 1984, color plate I. In *Cartier: The Cartier Room*, Grosvenor House Antiques
Fair, London, 1986, a wisteria and a geranium
plant, similar to the above were exhibited.

PLATE XXXV

MORNING GLORY

Rock crystal, aventurine quartz, ivory,
chalcedony, sapphire, moonstone, and silver.
circa 1926.

Ht. 10″ Base W. 6¼″
Ht. 25.4cm. W. 15.9cm.

A finely carved hardstone morning glory with rock crystal and aventurine flowers on a twisted oxidized silver stalk growing from aventurine quartz leaves and wrapped around an ivory bamboo pole. The plant sits in a white chalcedony framed smoky crystal tub containing aventurine quartz water and topped by four gold mounted cabochon sapphires. The whole is mounted on an ivory base enhanced with cabochon moonstone dewdrops.

Fabricator: Probably Fourrier Workshop,
        Saint-Siméon, Seine-et-Marne,
        for Cartier, Paris.

Cartier Stock Number: None.

Provenance: A La Vieille Russie, Inc., New York.
        The Lindemann Collection,
        New York, from 1987.

Comments:

The elegant stylization of the opening Morning Glory blossoms reflects both Louis Cartier's personal interest for the achitectonic and the tenets of the Art Deco manner. The piece is closely related in concept to Cartier's landscape-*cum*-animal sculptures (catalogue number XXIV) in which a total environment is implied. The inclusion of the moonstone dewdrops in the composition reinforces the image of the opening blossoms, compelling the viewer to sense the early morning, Post-dawn-moment of depiction. The capturing of a specific, yet transitory moment in nature is a feature of *ikebana*, indicating the fascination of the mature Art Deco period with the cultures of the Orient, and providing a contextual link between this sculpture and Cartier's other floral pieces.

Equally reflective of Cartier's personal taste is the apparently casual placement of the flowering vine about its leaning ivory "bamboo" stake. The configuration is thus seemingly simple but technically difficult to achieve. This off-center placement is a delightful contrast to the stark architecture of the slatted *jardinière*. In its overall effect of airy gracefulness, the Morning Glory recalls such floral works of Peter Carl Fabergé (1846-1920) as the spectacular "Lily-of-the-Valley" basket in the Matilda Geddings Gray Foundation Collection, New Orleans.

Fabergé also produced a Morning Glory for Queen Alexandra of England. However, the Fabergé interpretation featured a bold polychrome-enamelled silver single blossom whose vine was entwined around a silver pole. Typically, the Fabergé interpretation is smaller than this Cartier model.

Contrary to Cartier's usual practice with the floral pieces, which are usually unsigned, this sculpture bears a Chinese-styled chop mark signature on the plinth.

The Morning Glory is accompanied by its original satin lined flowered green paper-covered travelling case marked "Cartier, Paris 13 rue de la Paix, London, 4 New Burlington Street."

For further comments on Cartier's plant and flower sculptures, see catalogue numbers XXXI, XXXII, XXXIII, XXXIV, and XXXVI.

PLATE XXXVI

PAIR OF CACTI

Jade, moonstone, chalcedony, onyx, enamel, and gold.
circa 1925.

Ht. 5³/₄″ Diam. of Pot 4¹/₈″
Ht. 14.5cm. Diam. 10.5cm.

These plants are of eliptical carved jade with additional rounded jade appendages. One plant is set with blue and red enamel blossoms in a grey chalcedony pot enhanced with a cut ziggurat gold border and gold collet chalcedony cabochons. The other jade plant is set with moonstone and turquoise enamel blossoms in a black onyx pot, similarly shaped gold border and mounted black onyx cabochons.

Fabricator: Probably Fourrier Workshop,
       Saint-Siméon, Seine-et-Marne,
       for Cartier, Paris.

Cartier Stock Number: None.

Provenance: Auction: Christie's, Geneva, May 16,
       1985, #328, illustrated.
       The Lindemann Collection, New York,
       from 1985.

Comments:

Only two pair of these miniature sculptures are known to have been created. One pair was formerly in the collection of Mrs. Franklyn Hutton (née Marjorie Merriweather Post), from whom H. Robert Greene acquired it.

In contrast to the earlier Fabergé-inspired flower pieces, these delightful cacti were intended to be displayed without the traditional Cartier glass vitrine. The greenhouse case would have been illogical for a desert plant, and irrational to the Art Deco sensibility. As such, they are an excellent example of the sculptural qualities prevalent in Cartier's designs and are indicative of the strong three dimensional character preferred by the Lindemanns.

Cacti with their strong natural geometerical shapes were ideal subjects for Art Deco interpretation and provided a perfect palette for the inclusion of a number of influences. Akin to Cartier's Indo-Islamic range, the zig-zag design on the pots is reminiscent of the Mesopotamian ziggurat motif favored by Louis Cartier. Simultaneously, the color combinations of green and red and green and blue lend an air of Moghul opulence to the sculptures.

However, these charming cacti also exude the *ikebana*-inspired aura of transitoriness evident in Cartier's other floral pieces. Precipitation being a rare and sudden occurence in their natural environment, cacti bloom for only a moment. Cartier has captured with a charming quality the beauty of this brief moment.

For further comments on Cartier's plant and flower sculptures, see catalogue numbers XXXI, XXXII, XXXIII, XXXIV, and XXXV.

PLATE XXXVII

VASE

Lacque burgauté, gold, enamel, and silver.
1926.

Ht. 4³/₄″ W. 1⅝″ D. 1⅝″.
Ht. 12cm. W. 4.1cm. D. 4.1cm.

This vase gently flares from the square base towards a rounded top with a waisted neck. The sides are comprised of four arched *lacque burgauté* Chinese panels from the Ch'ing Dynasty (1644-1911) in Oriental landscape motifs bordered in gold. The top is silver enamelled black with a red neck whose base is enhanced by gold lambrequin borders.

Fabricator: Cartier, Paris.

Cartier Stock Number: #6940.

Provenance: Baron James Armand de Rothschild.
Obsidian, London.
The Lindemann Collection, New York, from 1983.

Comments:

According to the Cartier archives, this vase was one of thirty commissioned in 1926 by Baron James Armand de Rothschild (1878-1957) of Waddesdon Manor, Aylesbury, Buckinghamshire, as Christmas presents. There were four variations in the design of the vase. Of the thirty pieces originally commissioned, only one other is now known to exist; it is in the collection of the Musée Cartier, Geneva, Switzerland.

Like those of India, Egypt, and antiquity, Oriental motifs provided the basis for an entire range in the Cartier *oeuvre*. Though sometimes Japanese, most frequently the inspiration was derived from Chinese models.

The earliest reference to Chinese motifs pertains to a series of belt buckles created in 1898. Cartier had several other contacts with Chinese art throughout the Edwardian era; however, it was not until 1913 that the firm produced the first Chinese-inspired cigarette cases.

Following the same techniques the firm used to assimilate other non-European influences, Cartier systematically integrated Chinese influences into the Art Deco style. By 1930 elements such as *lacque burgauté*, *nacre*, lacquered woods, and Buddhist and Taoist imagery had become part of the Cartier Art Deco vocabulary.

This vase has been illustrated in: *I Gioielle Degli Anni '20-40 Cartier e i Grandi del Deco*, Palazzo Fortuny, Venice, 1986, plate 161; and *Cartier: The Cartier Room*, Grosvenor House Antiques Fair, London, 1986, #98.

For further comments on *lacque burgauté*, see catalogue numbers XXXVIII , and XXXIX.

For similar see *The H. Robert Greene Collection of Art Deco*, Christie's, Geneva, November 16, 1978; and the collection of the Musée Cartier, Geneva, Switzerland.

PLATE XXXVIII

TABLE CIGARETTE BOX

Nephrite, *lacque burgauté*, diamond, coral,
enamel, and gold.
1927.

Ht. 1½″ W. 5½″ D. 3⅛″
Ht. 4cm. W. 14cm. D. 8cm.

A table cigarette box carved from a single block of
nephrite. The lid is comprised of three *lacque burgauté* Chinese panels from the Ch'ing Dynasty
(1644-1911). Cabochon corals are set in each corner of the main panel. The entire lid is encased
within an 18 karat gold and black enamel border,
and further enhanced with gold palmettes. A coral,
black enamel, and rose diamond thumbpiece, and
other cabochon coral decoration on the rear section
of the hinge complete the design.

Fabricator: Coüet Workshop, Paris, for Cartier,
Paris.

Cartier Stock Number: #139.

Provenance: Cartier, Paris.
Mrs. J. Corrigan.
Obsidian, London.
The Lindemann Collection, New York,
from 1985.

Comments:

This rare and opulent table object is a fine example of the luxurious character of Cartier's functional pieces. It was the genius of Louis Cartier and
his designers to be able to lift a period element from
its original context and refashion it into a valid example of the Art Deco style. Typical of Art Deco
taste are the contrast of the dark nephrite with the
evanescent coloring of the *lacque burgauté*, the
coral baton-like thumbpiece with its contrasting
bands of black enamel and stylishly scrolled gold,
and the black enamel framing of the segmented lid.

Cartier had used mother-of-pearl inlays on objects as early as 1913. *Lacque burgauté*, a rare 18th

century lacquered mother-of-pearl, however, was
the first period Chinese element to be integrated in
Cartier's Art Deco designs. Taken from antique objects purchased from European dealers, the lustrous opalescent surface of *lacque burgauté*, often
enhanced with dyes, complemented the hardstone
and lacquered wood objects on which it was
placed. Cut up and set into the surfaces in Oriental
motifs, it was usually accented with cabochon
gems, bright enamels, palmette designs, and gold
inlays. The Taoist-inspired *chinoiserie* pieces created with this material became synonomous with
Art Deco and hallmarks of Cartier during the
1920s.

Originally, the palmettes on this box were coral.
In November 1931, Cartier modified the design and
replaced them with gold palmettes.

The box is signed "Cartier" on the gold mount
and is accompanied by its original fitted red leather
case which is also stamped "Cartier."

For further comments on *lacque burgauté*, see
catalogue numbers XXXVII and XXXIX.

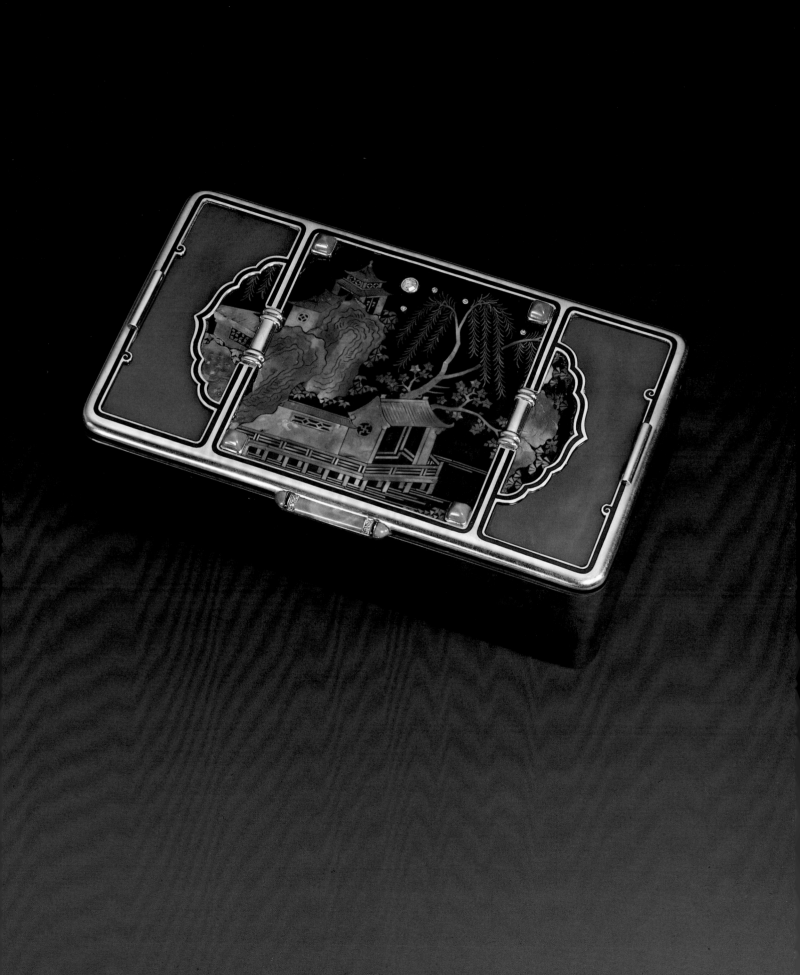

PLATE XXXIX

COMPACT

Amethyst, *lacque burgauté*, diamond, *nacre*,
sapphire, and gold.
circa 1927, *lacque burgauté*, 18th century.

Ht. ½″ W. 2 ⅛″ D. 2 ⅛″
Ht. 1.2cm. W. 5.4cm. D. 5.4cm.

A square-shaped compact with chamfered corners
in the Chinese style. The lid and base are set with
lacque burgaute plaques from the Ch'ing Dynasty
(1644-1911). The plaques are inlaid with *nacre* and
gold, and surrounded by a red enamel border with
nacre sections and rose diamond palmettes. The
sides are further adorned with similar borders
around sapphire and amethyst mosaics, centered
with a rose diamond push piece. The interior of this
case is fitted with the original *nacre* mesh powder
constrainer.

Fabricator: Cartier, Paris.

Cartier Stock Number: #5381.

Provenance: Obsidian, London.
The Lindemann Collection, New York,
from 1984.

Comments:

Compacts enjoyed increasing popularity in the
1920s and '30s as cosmetics and other fashion accessories, especially the handbag, came into
vogue. Cartier created a variety of these cases in
many different styles, often with matching lipsticks
and other personal items. This compact incorporates panels of *lacque burgauté* which was popularized in Cartier's Art Deco designs. While most
compacts were hinged, this unusual example is
composed of two parts which fit together to form an
Oriental-style box. Both the top and the bottom sections are decorated with the Taoist-inspired images
common to the *chinoiserie* idiom of Cartier.

This compact is accompanied by a fitted red
leather case.

For further comments on *lacque burgauté* see catalogue numbers XXXVII and XXXVIII.

For similar works see: "Cartier, Sovereign Jeweller", *Connoisseur*, November 1982; *I Gioielle Degli Anni '20-40 Cartier e i Grandi del Déco*, Palazzo
Fortuny, Venice, 1986; Nadelhoffer, H., *Cartier:
Jewelers Extraordinary*, Thames and Hudson,
1984; Raulet, S., *Art Deco Jewelry*, Thames and
Hudson, 1985; *Restrospective Louis Cartier, Masterworks of Art Deco*, Los Angeles County Museum,
1982-1983; and *Retrospective Louis Cartier, 101
Years of the Jeweler's Art*, Cartier, New York, 1976.

PLATE XL

CIGARETTE CASE

Jade, *nacre*, enamel, gold, and mirror.
circa 1927.

Ht.½″ W. 3 ⅝″ D. 1 ⅞″
Ht. 1.5cm. W. 9cm. D. 5cm.

A flat rectangular 18 karat gold cigarette case with a concealed opening mechanism. The lid and reverse contain simulated lapis-lazuli enamelled panels. The panels are bordered on either end with *pavé*-set rose diamond edged with gold mounted and engraved *nacre*, and arrow-shaped black enamel and rose diamond decoration. The sides of the case are set with batons of pale green jade. The interior is fitted with a compartment for cigarettes and a bevelled mirror.

Fabricator: Cartier, Paris.

Cartier Stock Number: Number illegible.

Provenance: Auction: Christie's, New York, April 24, 1985, #114, color illustration.
Obsidian, London.
The Lindemann Collection, New York, from 1985.

Comments:

Although Cartier had been producing smoker's requisites since the 1880s, with the advent of the capacious handbag and general acceptance of public smoking in the 1920s, items such as the cigarette case became popular accessories. The case was often part of a coordinated set with a matching lighter, lipstick, compact, and other personal items, an ensemble that made a perfect fashion statement.

This unusual case is equipped with an elaborate opening mechanism which is activated by the application of pressure to the jade batons at either side. This mechanical complexity is matched by panels of exquisite *faux*-lapis enamel on the lid and bottom. The opulent combination of genuine and simulated luxury materials is characteristic of Cartier's best work during the late 1920s.

Similar cases are illustrated in: Gautier, G., *Cartier, The Legend*, Arlington Books, 1984; Nadelhoffer, H., *Cartier: Jewelers Extraordinary*, Thames and Hudson, 1984; *Retrospective Louis Cartier, Masterworks of Art Deco*, Los Angeles County Museum, 1982-1983; and *Retrospective Louis Cartier, 101 Years of the Jeweler's Art*, Cartier, New York, 1976.

PLATE XLI

FRAME

Agate, coral, diamond, onyx, enamel, gold, and
silver-gilt.
circa 1927.

Ht. 10 $\frac{1}{8}$" W. 8 $\frac{1}{4}$"
Ht. 25.7cm. W. 20.9cm.

An upright rectangular agate frame with a black
and red enamelled inner border. The border is broken at the top by a carved coral flower set in gold,
rimmed with black enamel and accented with *pavé*-
set rose diamonds. The frame is enhanced by corner guards of red enamel on gold in an Oriental motif *pavé*-set with rose diamonds and cabochon
black onyx. A rose diamond cipher is located at the
bottom center of the frame. The back is fitted with
a silver-gilt easel.

Fabricator: Cartier, Paris.

Cartier Stock Number: #1500.

Provenance: Obsidian, London.
　　　　　　The Lindemann Collection, New
　　　　　　York, from 1982.

Comments:

The popular photograph frame of the 1920s and
'30s was an excellent subject for the application of
Louis Cartier's "functional jewel" concept. Its obvious use and simple basic shape which was malleable and could be manipulated to suit any theme
appealed to Art Deco taste. Cartier employed a variety of materials to create several stunning examples which reflect influences similar to those
apparent in the concurrent designs for jewelry and
other *objets de vertu.*

Typical of Cartier's work during the "Golden
Era" years, *circa* 1919-1939, the design of this
elaborate frame exudes an air of Moghul opulence.

The Oriental flavor of the red, gold, and black color
combination is enhanced by the use of carved coral
which recalls the flower cults of the Moghul emper-
ors, and by the Persian-styled motifs on the corners. Simultaneously, the contrast of softly glowing
onyx, translucent agate, glittering diamonds, and
glistening polychrome enamels typifies the striking
contrasts favored in the Art Deco mode.

The photograph is of Mrs. George Lindemann
and her daughter, Sloan, taken at The Lido in Venice in 1977.

For further comments and comparison, see catalogue numbers XX, XXVIII, and LI.

PLATE XLII

CIGAR BOX WITH CLOCK

Silver, gold, *nacre*, and jade.
circa 1927.

Ht. 2 ⅞″ W. 7 ⅝″ D. 3 ⅜″
Ht. 7.3cm. W. 19.4cm. D. 8.5cm.

A rectangular polished silver box with mahogany interior lining and feet. The stepped lid centers upon a jade and mother-of-pearl dial with gold Roman numerals, flanked on three sides by stepped and carved jade motifs trimmed in yellow gold.

Fabricator: Cartier, Paris.

Cartier Stock Number: #2592.

Provenance: Auction: Christie's, New York, March 5, 1985, #205, illustrated.
The Lindemann Collection, New York, from 1985.

Comments:

One of the influences upon the Art Deco style was ancient Near Eastern architecture, particularly the ziggurat whose stepped form is reflected in the lid of this box. The emergent style, as seen at the influential Paris *Exposition Internationale des Arts décoratifs et industriels modernes* in 1925, favored a sleek geometry, often arranged in an architectonic fashion. Typical of Cartier designs of this type during the late 1920s, the clock is further refined by hinges so that it may be displayed vertically. So displayed, its effect is yet more architectural.

As Hans Nadelhoffer points out, these architecture-influenced utilitarian objects frequently had their severity modified by the use of mother-of-pearl inlays and other elements. This tempering of pure Art Deco style is seen here in the *nacre* dial of the clock. (Nadelhoffer, H., *Cartier: Jewelers Extraordinary*, Harry N. Abrams, New York, 1984. p. 201.)

A similar silver cigar box, formerly in the collection of William Randolph Hearst, San Simeon, California, was in the collection of H. Robert Greene, and is illustrated in the Greene Collection Auction catalogue, Christie's, Geneva, November 16, 1978. However, the Hearst-Greene cigar box is not so architectural in form.

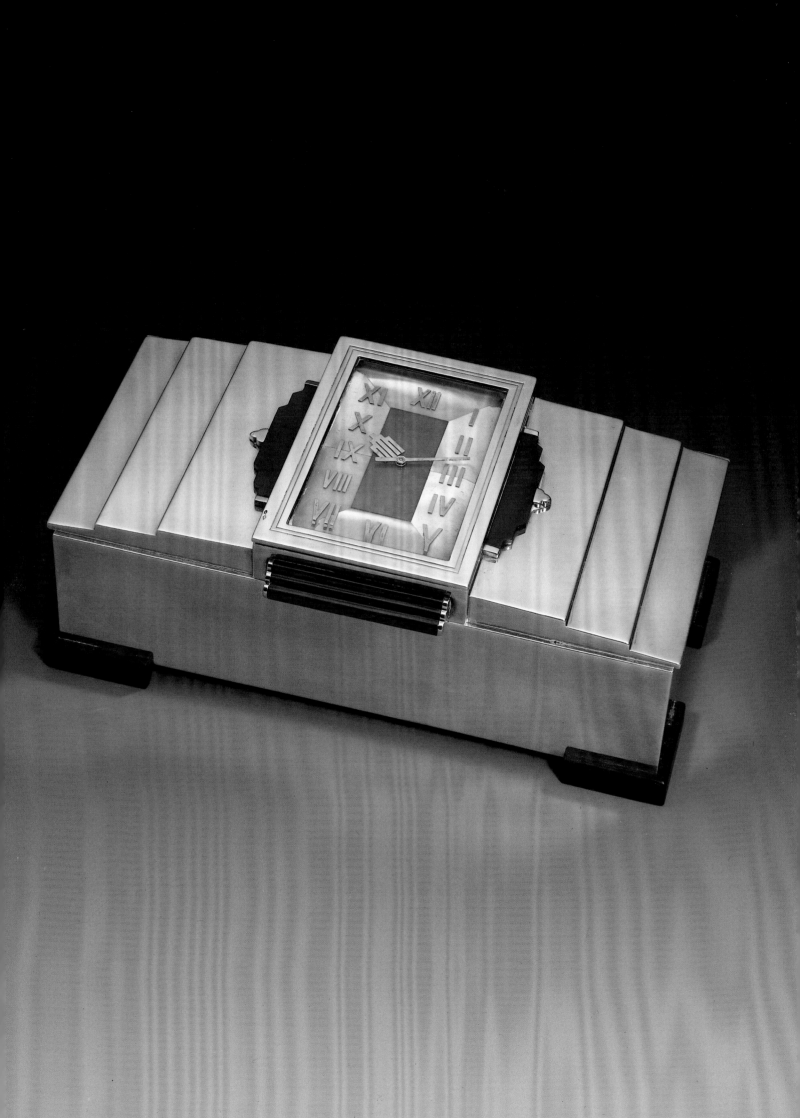

PLATE XLIII

TABLE CIGARETTE BOX

Alabaster, coral, emerald, enamel, and gold.
1928.

Ht. 2″ W. 5″ D. 3 ¼″
Ht. 5.1cm. W. 12.8cm. D. 8.3cm.

A flat rectangular carved alabaster box with scalloped feet. Its lid is mounted with two red coral batons attached at opposite ends of the hinge side. Each baton is banded with two black enamel on gold rings, and further enhanced with gold collet cabochon emerald butts. A coral annulus handle is secured to the front by a black enamel bail. The hinges are in polished 18 karat gold.

Fabricator: Coüet Workshop, Paris, for Cartier, Paris.

Cartier Stock Number: #216.

Provenance: Auction: Christie's, New York, October 22, 1985, #24, illustrated. The Lindemann Collection, New York, from 1985.

Comments:

The European fascination with the Egyptian motifs apparent in many Art Deco designs was not unique, but an interest which evolved through many phases. This interest had its roots in the late eighteenth century when under the rule of Napoléon Bonaparte Egyptian decor pervaded designs in many of the decorative arts. It continued to be stimulated throughout the nineteenth century by a series of archeological discoveries and exhibitions. The discovery of King Tutankhamun's tomb in 1922 by Lord Carnarvon renewed this infatuation which culminated in the "Tutmania" of the 1920s and directly influenced the development of the international Art Deco style.

The simple bold outlines of this handsome box recall the alabaster caskets and containers found in the tomb of Tutankhamun. The stark contrast of white, coral, and black, while ancient Egyptian in appearance, was also very much within the perimeters of Louis Cartier's personal taste. He favored such contrasts, particularly when fabricated from fine and costly materials.

For further comments and comparison, see catalogue numbers XLIV and LV.

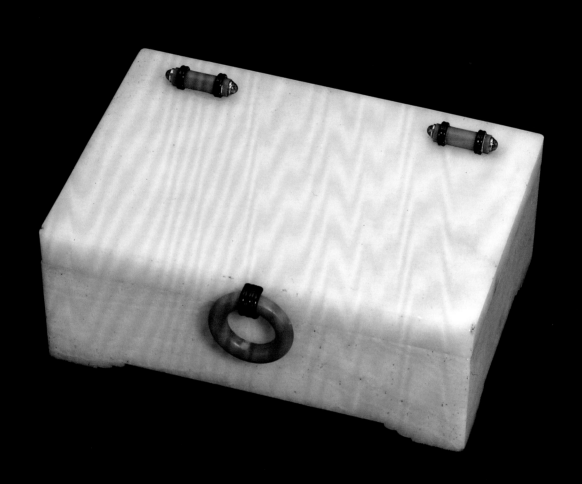

PLATE XLIV

LIPSTICK CASE

Pearl, turquoise, lapis-lazuli, diamond, enamel,
and gold.
circa 1928.

L. 2 ¼"
L. 5.8 cm.

This piece is designed in the shape of an Egyptian
canopic jar. The body is inlaid with zig-zag patterns of turquoise and lapis-lazuli, and bordered
with small gold bands. Diamonds *pavé*-set in patterns of triangles, bands, and tear drops adorn the
top and bottom. Both ends are further enhanced
with pearls.

Fabricator: Lavabre Workshop, Paris, for Cartier,
Paris.

Cartier Stock Number: #0136.

Provenance: Auction: Sotheby's, St. Moritz,
February 19-21, 1987, #545,
illustrated.
The Lindemann Collection, New
York, from 1987.

Comments:

Cartier had experimented with Egyptian-in-
spired motifs since the beginning; the earliest
pieces by the firm date back to 1852. The interest
for such works ebbed and waned with current
styles, but finally peaked in the early decades of
this century in the craze brought about by the discovery of King Tutankhamun's tomb by Lord Carnarvon in 1922. During the 1920s and '30s Cartier
designed many objects which incorporated the
shapes, patterns, and color schemes of Pharoanic
Egypt.

This lipstick case is modelled after the traditional Egyptian canopic, or funerary, jar. The motifs here and their palette recall the appearance of
ancient Egyptian glass and faïence while remaining
well within the tenets of Art Deco taste. Such small
stylish pieces were usually made with other matching handbag or cosmetic accessories.

The compact matching this lipstick case is in the
collection of the Musée Cartier, Geneva, Switzerland.

The piece is accompanied by a fitted red leather
case.

It is illustrated in color in Raulet, S., *Bijoux Art
Déco*, Editions du Regard, 1984, page 272.

For further comments and comparison, see catalogue numbers XLIII and LV.

PLATE XLV

VANITY/LIPSTICK

Sapphire, diamond, turquoise, enamel, and gold. circa 1928-1932.

Vanity L. 3″ Lipstick L. 2″
Vanity L. 7.7cm. Lipstick L. 5cm.

The tapered cylinder of the lipstick is opaque white enamel on gold accented with thin gold rings and a central band of *pavé*-set diamonds. Gold collet cabochon sapphires ornament the ends of the tube. The flat rectangular compact is also opaque white enamel on gold; the top edges and hinges are defined with ribbons of *pavé*-set diamonds. The hinges are further enhanced with *pavé*-set brilliant and rose diamond arrows. The top of the case is gold rimmed adorned with stylized arrowhead form strapwork in *pavé*-set rose diamond with channel-set baton turquoise, square cabochon sapphires, and a diamond-shaped cabochon turquoise. A square cabochon sapphire accents the top at each end of the arrowhead.

Fabricator: Cartier, New York.

Cartier Stock Number: None.

Provenance: Lilyan S. Lindemann (Mrs. Joseph S. Lindemann), New York.
The Lindemann Collection, New York, from 1986.

Comments:

The vanity, or *nécessaire*, became extremely popular in the 1920s, and remained so until the appeal of the more capacious handbag superceded it in the '30s. The production of the vanity continued, however, through World War II, although the form was considerably altered into a pouch shape.

The form of the early vanity cases and lipsticks was adapted by Louis Cartier from the traditional Japanese *inro*, a masculine accoutrement suspended from the kimono sash (*obi*) and containing drugs or medicine. The cord from which the *inro* was suspended was terminated by a carved button (*netsuke*). In this case the *netsuke* became the lipstick, which though now separate, was originally attached to the vanity by a fine gold chain. Other such vanities terminated in a circular hardstone finger ring. This adaptation is one of the relatively rare direct influences of Japanese art upon the creations of Cartier.

Constructed in the tradition of these early Cartier vanities, the adornment of this example reflects a transition between the first and second phase of the Art Deco mode. In contrast to the former, the second phase was characterized by larger, more chunky, flattened and severely geometrical shapes as can be seen in the abstracted central arrow form on the top of this case. The smaller ribbon-like decorations are more representative of the earlier phase of the style. Here though, they too have been treated with a heightened emphasis on their simple angular traits.

For further comments, see catalogue numbers XXVII, and L.

PLATE XLVI

POWDER COMPACT

Diamond, emerald, enamel, platinum, and gold.
circa 1928.

Diam. 2¹/₂″
Diam. 6. 3cm.

A small circular compact. The exterior is edged in blue *guilloché* enamel. The lid and underside are cream enamel stripes over gold. The center of the lid is decorated with a *pavé*-set "Tree of Life" motif in rose diamonds and stylized cabochon emerald "fruits" set in platinum collets, against a geometric design in blue *guilloché* enamel. The interior is fitted as a single compartment.

Fabricator: Cartier, New York.

Cartier Stock Number: #4085.

Provenance: Obsidian, London.
　　　　　　The Lindemann Collection, New
　　　　　　York, from 1984.

Comments:

Cartier had produced powder compacts from its early years. Make-up, however, was generally frowned upon throughout the nineteenth century and did not become fashionable until the cosmetics vogue of the 1920s. Even then, the popularity of stylishly appointed individual personal items was for a time superceded by the vanity which combined a host of these objects into one unit. With the advent of the handbag, however, the production of these singular items received the full attention of Cartier designers, who lavished their surfaces with gem-set decorations in all the current motifs.

As with those of his other Art Deco creations, Louis Cartier's designs for compacts often incorporated elements of ancient and eastern art coupled with the tenets of his personal taste. In this compact Cartier combined Art Deco geometry with his affinity for naturalistic subject matter and popular Indo-Islamic influences in order to create a functional case possessing elegance and a daring use of shape, content, and color.

This compact is accompanied by the original powder block.

A similar compact is illustrated in Nadelhoffer, H., *Cartier: Jewelers Extraordinary*, Thames and Hudson, 1984, plate 32.

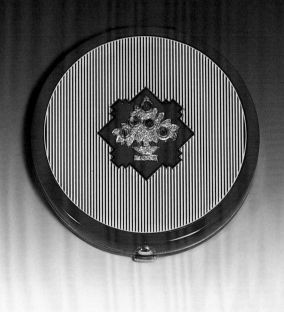

PLATE XLVII

LETTER KNIFE

Agate, kingfisher feathers, lapis-lazuli, sapphire, gold, and silver.
circa 1930.

L. 12½"
L. 31 .8cm.

A large lancet ended agate paper knife. The smooth blade gently tapers toward a silver encased clock handle. The dial is applied iridescent king fisher feathers, with gold colored Roman chapters. It is surrounded with an 18 karat gold bezel and accented with channel-set baton lapis-lazuli motifs on the shaft and butt, a carved lapis-lazuli wind stem, and a cabochon sapphire collet. The reverse side is engraved with the monogram "ELD."

Fabricator: Cartier, Paris.

Cartier Stock Number: #1987.

Provenance: The Vincentian Fathers and Brothers.
Auction: Christie's, New York,
September 10, 1985, #15,
illustrated.
The Lindemann Collection, New
York, from 1985.

Comments:

The use of brilliant blue kingfisher feathers as a ground was adapted by Louis Cartier from its employ on antique Chinese hair ornaments and picture grounds, and was utilized by the firm from 1920. Here the feathers have been laid to create a basket-weave central panel in the clock dial, each end of which is flanked by smaller panels with tangent demilune feathers. The shimmering blue of the feathers provides an elegant counterpoint to the opaque blue of the six lapis-lazuli batons, the gleaming single cabochon sapphire, and the translucent agate of the blade.

Such dual function objects were much admired during the heyday of the Art Deco style, the influences of which are apparent in the modeling of the chapters, the sleek gentle swelling of the clock case, and the scalloped lambrequin-like shaping at the join of the clock and blade.

For a similar paper cutter with watch see *Retrospective Louis Cartier, 101 Years of the Jeweler's Art,* Cartier, New York, 1976, plate 40.

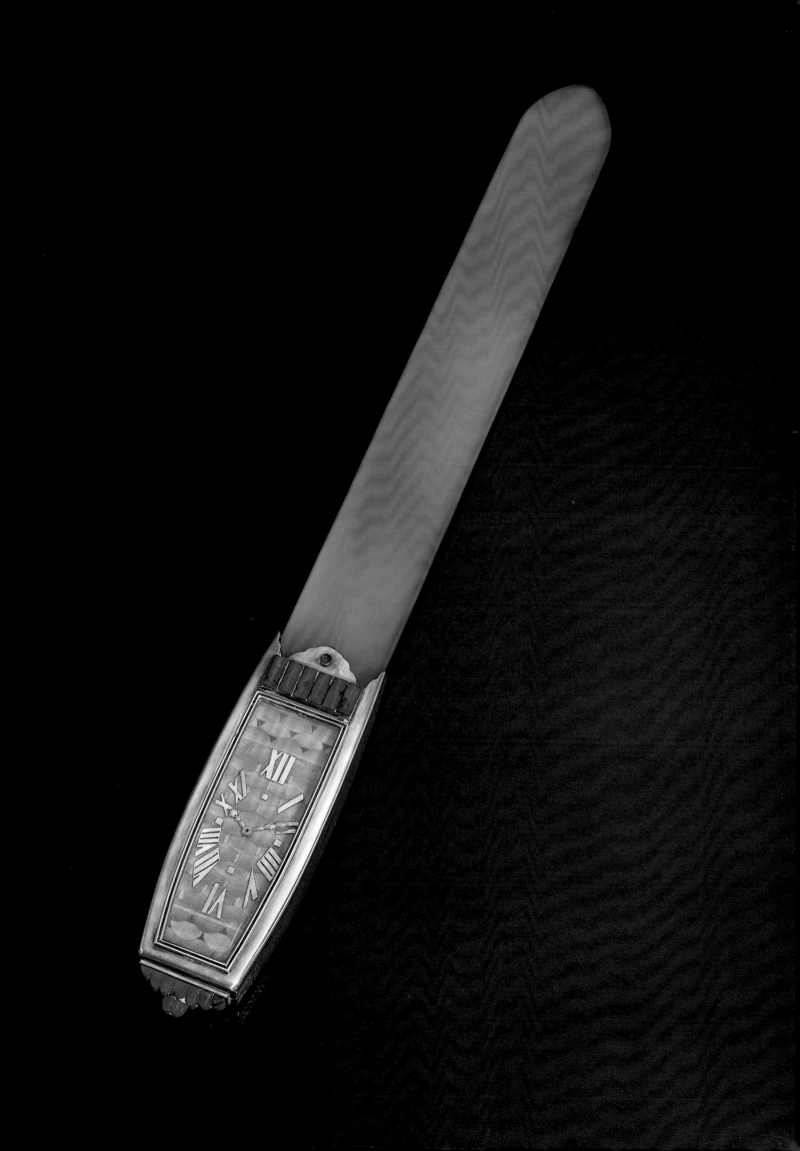

PLATE XLVIII

CIGAR BOX

Moss agate, moonstone, enamel, and gold.
circa 1930.

Ht. 1½″ W. 7⅛″ D. 3⅝″
Ht. 3.8cm. W. 18.1cm. D. 9.2cm.

A flat rectangular box of carved moss agate; the hinges and clasp of gold, enamelled with opaque white, and set with triangular cabochon moonstones. The clasp is further enhanced with square cabochon moonstones in gold collets in an interlaced Arabic strapwork design of white enamel on gold.

Fabricator: Cartier, Paris.

Cartier Stock Number: None.

Provenance: Auction: Sotheby's, Geneva,
November 12, 1986, #320,
illustrated.
The Lindemann Collection, New
York, from 1986.

Comments:

Cartier's Art Deco designs were often inspired by Near Eastern art. In this box, the influence of Indo-Islamic trellis-work and star patterns is evident in the adornment. The use of such "structural" ornaments for hinges and clasps was popularized by Cartier designer, Charles Jacqueau (1885-1968), and represent a quintessential element of the functional aesthetic within the Art Deco style. Here the functional lattice designs have been combined with an unusually subtle contrast of colors to create a lyrical composition in which the wavy characteristics of the translucent moss agate are highlighted and complemented by the pale lavender moonstones and simple opaque white enamel patterns.

This box is accompanied by its original fitted red leather case.

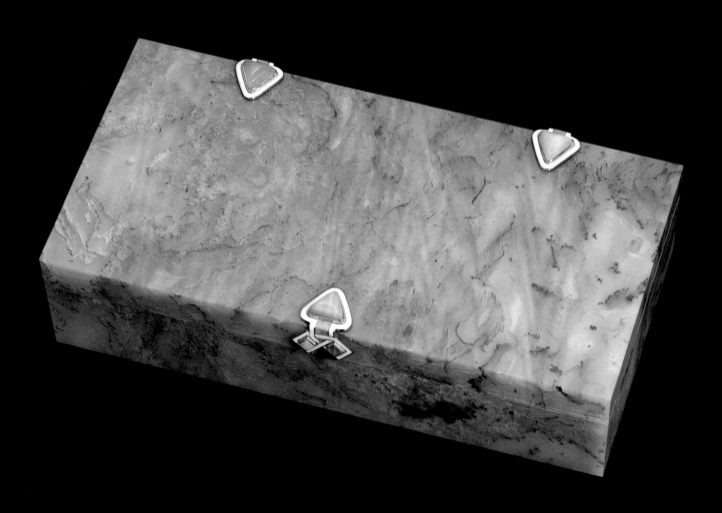

PLATE XLIX

LARGE CASKET

Brown agate, nephrite, coral, enamel, and gold.
circa 1930.

Ht. 3″ W. 8³/₈″ D. 5″
Ht. 7.6cm. W. 21.3cm. D. 12.7cm.

A large rectangular carved brown agate box, the
edges and corners of which are framed in incised
gold. The lid is decorated with a floral basket motif.
A baton nephrite in gold collet basket holds large
gold collet cabochon coral flowers with blue enamel
on gold leaves and smaller floral patterns in gold
with red enamel. The design is completed with a
gold serpentine thumbpiece.

Fabricator: Cartier, Paris.

Cartier Stock Number: None.

Provenance: Mrs. Franklyn Hutton. (née, Marjorie
          Merriweather Post)
          H. Robert Greene, New York.
          Auction: *The H. Robert Greene
          Collection of Art Deco*, Christie's,
          Geneva, November 16, 1978.
          The Lindemann Collection, New
          York, from 1982.

Comments:

   Containers such as this were popular Art Deco
table and desk ornaments and were used for a variety of functions from cigar and cigarette boxes to
jewel cases and valets. Towards the end of the
1920s the sizes of such boxes increased, reflecting
not only a change in purpose but also the evolving
interests which characterize the second phase of
the Art Deco mode. In contrast to the earlier designs, those of the second phase emphasized larger
shapes, a more severe geometry, and the use of
boldly stylized adornment. The flattened spray of
berries in a basket on this exquisite example is typical of the more monumental scale favored by Art
Deco designers during the 1930s. In addition, the
subtle shadings of the primary agate panels function as perfect foils for the more vivid hues of coral
and nephrite accented with glistening red and blue
enamel. The effect finally achieved is one of a softly
glowing understated opulence.

PLATE L

VANITY

Diamond, onyx, enamel, and gold.
circa 1931-1932.

L. 3¼"
L. 8.2cm.

A compressed cylindrical case designed in the Art Deco style. The case is gold with fine black enamel stripes on the top and sides, and has black enamel ends. The edges and centers of the ends are enhanced with narrow rings of *pavé*-set rose diamonds. The case is attached on one end to a black onyx annulus finger ring by means of two chains, each comprised of two elongated black enamel links joined to the ends of a rose diamond-capped onyx baton. Attached to opposite sides of the case, these chains join the finger ring at a band of alternating *pavé*-set rose diamond and black enamel rings.

Fabricator: Cartier, London.

Cartier Stock Number: None.

Provenance: Lilyan S. Lindemann (Mrs. Joseph S. Lindemann), New York.
The Lindemann Collection, New York, from 1984.

Comments:

Although its popularity was eventually superseded by the handbag, Cartier continued producing vanities in various forms through the Second World War. The basic designs of 1930s differed little from those executed earlier in the heyday of the vanity during the '20s. Like their predecessors, the *inro* commonly worn by Japanese men served as their inspiration. Cartier's designs, however, were used by women and included compartments for powder, rouge and cigarettes. The cases were attached by chain to a finger ring. An alternative form was a lipstick case which bore similar mountings.

One notable change between the design for vanities of the two decades is exhibited by this elegant example. Vanities created in the 1920s reflected a variety of exotic and at times fanciful motifs, such as stylized arabesques (catalogue number XXVII) and figures. In contrast, the designs of the 1930s emphasize the bold geometrization popular in the second phase of the Art Deco mode. This trend is reflected in this case by simple linear aspects which reiterate and accentuate the basic shape of the case.

For further comments, see catalogue numbers, XXVII and XLV.

PLATE LI

FRAME

Lapis-lazuli, sapphire, gold, and wood.
circa 1947-1948.

Ht. 12³/₈″ W. 8″
Ht. 31.5cm. W. 20.3cm

An elongated rectangular frame executed in gold. The sides are ribbed and joined at simple square plaques. The frame is enhanced with a decoration of criss-crossed lapis-lazuli batons set with gold stars and flanked by gold collet cabochon sapphires. This frame is backed with light colored maghogany.

Fabricator: Cartier, New York.

Cartier Stock Number: None.

Provenance: Lilyan S. Lindemann (Mrs. Joseph S. Lindemann), New York.
The Lindemann Collection, New York, from 1982.

Comments:

As had earlier been the practice of the Russian court jeweler, Peter Carl Fabergé (1846-1920), the House of Cartier produced photograph frames in a wide variety of models. The photograph, even as late as the 1930s, was still something of a novelty and a fashionable interior ornament.

After thirty years of being secondary to platinum, gold became increasingly popular again during the chaotic post-war years. The trend of using gold liberally in designs for jewelry and *objets de vertu* began during World War II and continued afterwards. Lacking the flexibility of platinum, objects made of gold were necessarily less heavily adorned with small gems. Fortunately, this quality was well suited to the chunky geometric designs of the Art Moderne style which was coming into vogue at the time.

The design of this photograph frame with its simply adorned gold surface and severe angular shape exhibits traits admired in the new style. The traditional outlines in this case, however, reflect the classical shapes and imagery preferred by many governmental agencies, especially the military.

Cartier had produced several designs for Charles de Gaulle, head of the French Provisional Government prior to the end of the war. With the allied victory, some of these designs were applied to medals and awards for military achievement. The possibility that this frame was intended for a similar honor is evidenced by the lapis-lazuli batons at the top. Traditionally carried by leaders, such batons have become the particular distinction of field marshalls in this century.

The photograph in this frame is of George Lindemann, with the French stallion I Love You taken in 1985.

For further comments and comparison, see catalogue numbers XX, XXVIII, and XLI.

CLOCKS, WATCHES, AND INSTRUMENTS

PLATE LII

REPEATER CLOCK

Seed pearl, diamond, grey agate, enamel, silver, and rock crystal.
1899.

Ht. 3″ W. 1¾″ D. 1½″
Ht. 7.6cm. W. 4.4cm. D. 3.8 cm.

An upright rectangular-shaped case in white trimmed powder blue *guilloché* enamel in a moiré pattern on a carved grey agate base. The case is mounted with a round white enamel dial with gold rose diamond set pointers, and black enamel Arabic chapters. The dial is enhanced with a seed pearl studded gold bezel holding a rock crystal lunette glass. A rock crystal plunger tops the case.

Fabricator: Cartier, Paris.

Cartier Stock Number: Numbered inside clock case.

Provenance: Le Vieux Paris, New York.
The Lindemann Collection, New York, from 1983.

Comments:

The form of this table clock recalls that of the eighteenth-century carriage clock, with the notable exception of the replacement of the traditional carriage clock's bail handle by a circular rock crystal plunger.

Late nineteenth-century taste distinctly favored historicizing French style and such delicate colors and muted borders as the pearl studded bezel of the clock face. These compositions reflect the style of late eighteenth-century enamelled snuffboxes and *bonbonières*, which were widely admired and collected at the end of the century.

Such clocks had only recently been the arena of Fabergé. Louis Cartier greatly admired these delicately hued and finely crafted Russian objects and lavished brilliant blues, lavenders, Empire greens, and pink enamels on his silver-cased clocks. These *guilloché* enamels were sometimes referred to as "Russian" enamels. Fine as these enamels were, however, Cartier and his *ateliers* felt they were competing against a craft which had reached its apogee in Tsarist Russia.

Repeater clocks of this rectangular form were favored gifts during the early Edwardian era (1901-1910); from 1908, they were joined by a circular model, and an arched version was added in 1909.

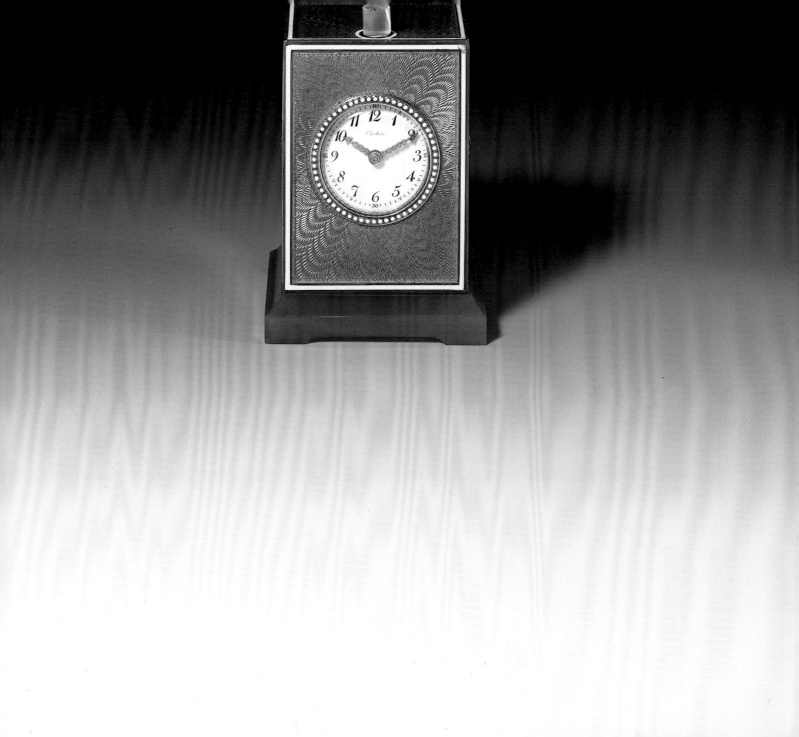

PLATE LIII

ALARM CLOCK

Agate, sapphire, gold, enamel, and silver.
circa 1908.

Ht. 4 ¼″ W. 2 ⅜″ D. 2″
Ht. 10.8cm. W. 6.5cm. D. 5.1cm.

A upright rectangular-shaped case in white trimmed royal blue *guilloché* enamel over silver on a similarly trimmed violet sunray *guilloché* enamel base with gold disc feet enhanced with green and white enamel on gold wreath decoration. The case is mounted with a round white enamel dial with two black enamel chapter rings and gold pointers. The inner chapter ring in Roman numerals registers the passing hours; the outer, in Arabic numerals, the minutes. The dial is further accented with a white enamel-on-gold bezel which holds the rock crystal lunette glass. Centered atop the case is an annular agate finger ring secured to the case by a gold cube enhanced with cabochon sapphires.

Fabricator: Bako Workshop, Paris, for Cartier Paris.

Cartier Stock Number: #150.

Provenance: Auction: Christie's, New York, October 22, 1987, #5, illustrated. The Lindemann Collection, New York, from 1987.

Comments:

Such small table and boudoir clocks were admired internationally and were a favored present or friendship gift throughout the Edwardian era (1901-1910).

The chaste architectonic form here recalls, in simplified terms, mantelclocks of the Louis XVI period and, simultaneously, anticipate the severe geometrization of the approaching Art Deco style. Such enamelled clocks had been the preserve of the Russian, Peter Carl Fabergé (1846-1920), until Louis Cartier became interested in attempting to ri-val them; upon his examples, Cartier spread the brilliant enamels seen here. He also developed elaborate *guilloché* grounds such as the one ornamenting the body of this alarm clock. These were not infrequently further enhanced with mottoes in diamonds. *"L'amitié vous l'offre"* or *"le temps passe; les pensées restent"* were among the favored themes. Such fashion-setting clients as King Edward VII of England, Prince Constantin Radziwill, and Princess Zenaïde Youssoupov were among the many admirers of these early Cartier clocks.

The Bako *atelier*, which furnished this clock to Cartier, specialized in the production of finely enamelled small objects.

Similar clocks are illustrated in: *Magnificent Jewels*, Christie's, Geneva, April 27, 1978, #268, and *Retrospective Louis Cartier, Masterworks of Art Deco*, Cartier, New York, 1982, #39.

PLATE LIV

CURVIMETER

Seed pearl, enamel, and gold.
circa 1911.

L. (without chain) 1 ⁷⁄₈″ L. 4.8cm.

A pyriform 18 karat gold case decorated with a white enamel border, a "P" monogram surmounted by a coronet and mounted with a white enamel dial with black enamel numerals. The whole is suspended from a 14 karat gold and enamel chain formed of alternating white enamel bugle links and seed pearls.

Fabricator: Cartier, London.

Cartier Stock Number: #3738.

Provenance: Auction: Christie's, New York, October 22, 1985, #13, illustrated. The Lindemann Collection, New York, from 1985.

Comments:

An unusual object, the curvimeter measures distances on a map or a globe. As the small basal wheel is moved along a particular route. The dial registers the distance in miles or kilometers. Following in the tradition established by Fabergé, this utilitarian object has been transformed by its ornament into a decorative work of art.

The curvimeter is accompanied by its original fitted red leather case.

PENDANT WATCH

Jade, enamel, gold, and silk cording.
circa 1928.

Diam. ⁷⁄₈″ Cord L. 18″, Diam. 2.2cm. L. 45.7cm.

An 18 karat gold case decorated with red and black enamel. The case is mounted with a circular white enamel dial with black Roman numerals and Breguet pointers. A carved triple jade bow is hinged to the pendant and attached to a black silk cord enhanced with a pale green jade button and gold ornaments.

Fabricator: Cartier, Paris.

Cartier Stock Number: #83-1.

Provenance: Auction: Christie's, New York, October 22, 1985, #23, illustrated. The Lindemann Collection, New York, from 1985.

Comments:

Pendant watches made their initial appearance prior to World War I; however, it was during the 1920s that they became extremely modish costume accessories. This pendant watch epitomizes Art Deco taste of the late 1920s. Its multiple function as a necklace and a timepiece and its color scheme which are practical, yet daring, are hallmarks of the style. The simple geometry of circles and rings appealed to then contemporary taste, which required svelte outline and favored such striking contrasts as the jade, red enamel, and black silk cording.

The movement of this watch was made for Cartier by LeCoultre.

A nearly identical watch is illustrated in *Retrospective Louis Cartier, 101 Years of the Jeweler's Art,* Cartier, New York, 1976, plate 10.

Pocket Watch on page 176

PLATE LV

OBELISK CLOCK

Marble, diamond, gold, enamel, and platinum.
circa 1915.

Ht. 15 ¼″ W. 2⁵/₁₆″ D. 2⁵/₁₆″
Ht. 38.7cm. W. 6.8cm. D. 6.8cm.

A large marble obelisk, pedestal, and base. The pedestal is mounted with a square opalescent sunray *guilloché* enamel dial with gold rose diamond set pointers. The square chapter ring is white enamel with black enamel Roman numerals. The flat rock crystal glass is held by an accenting gold bezel. The entire piece is ribbon-bound with green and white enamel-on-gold bands. The upper band, decorating the obelisk at the top of the pedestal, is of neoclassical laurel leaves; the lower is a pellet molding adorning the pedestal at the base.

Fabricator: Coüet Workshop, Paris, for Cartier,
Paris.

Cartier Stock Number: #148.

Provenance: Private Collection, 1910.
H. Robert Greene, New York.
Auction: *The H. Robert Greene
Collection of Art Deco*, Christie's,
Geneva, November 16, 1978, #521,
color illustration.
Obsidian, London.
Private Collection, Paris.
Obsidian, London.
The Lindemann Collection, New
York, from 1986.

Comments:

This clock reflects the tastes of its day while simultaneously indicating the future of Cartier designs. The enamelled borders and opalescent dial are traditional elements associated with the "garland" style. However, their stylized treatment combined with the obvious Egyptian influences, the simple geometric emphasis, and a heightened sense of color, clearly mark this clock as an intermediate in the transition to the Art Deco style.

The craze for *égyptérie* was revived during the second half of the nineteenth century, and increased with each new archeological discovery. The obelisk had been a fashionable motif since the opening years of the nineteenth century. The obelisk emerged as a fashionable form during the Egyptian campaign of Napoléon Bonaparte and became a basic motif of the so-called *retour d'Egypte* style popular from 1805-1815. The revival of First Empire taste during the late years of the reign of Emperor Napoléon III provided added impetus to the popularity of such motifs. This revival was due both to the family connection of the third Napoléon to the "little Corsican" and to such engineering marvels as the Suez Canal.

By 1915, the craze was considerably influencing every aspect of fashion and the decorative arts, and was furthered by the 1922 discovery of King Tutankhamun's tomb by Lord Carnarvon. From this point on, Cartier began incorporating Egyptian motifs and color schemes freely into his designs. This inventive concept led to the startling synthesis of ancient and non-European art unique to the Art Deco style.

For further comments and comparison, see catalogue numbers XLIII and XLIV.

PLATE LVI

DESK CLOCK

Rose quartz, lapis-lazuli, diamond, *nacre*,
enamel, and gold.
circa 1920.

Ht. 3″ W. 2 ½″ D. 1 ⅛″
Ht. 7.6cm. W. 6.4cm. D. 2.8cm.

A bevelled square rose quartz case with chamfered
corners, mounted with a round inlaid *nacre* dial
with gold rose diamond set pointers. The chapter
ring is lapis-lazuli with applied gold Roman numerals. The dial is enhanced with a white enamel-
on-gold rope twist bezel holding a rock crystal lunette glass. The case is topped by a lapis-lazuli baton held by two posts embellished with alternating
black enamel and gold stripes.

Fabricator: Cartier, New York.

Cartier Stock Number: None.

Provenance: Cartier, New York.
          The Lindemann Collection, New
          York, from 1985.

Comments:

   Art Deco taste required an object to possess a
function beyond that of mere decorativeness. In this
light, a jeweled table ornament that was also a clock
could justify the expense of such an object. In this
clock, Cartier contrasted the luminiscence of rose
quartz and *nacre* against the deep luster of lapis-lazuli. Although the color scheme, the geometric
compactness of its form, and boldly modeled bail
handle firmly link this clock to the tenets of the Art
Deco manner, it nonetheless owes a debt to the soft
evanescent colors of the earlier Art Nouveau and
Edwardian tastes.

PLATE LVII

ALTAR CLOCK

Onyx, diamond, ruby, enamel, gold, and
platinum.
1928.

Ht. 2 ¾″ W. 2 ⅛″ D. 1 ½″
Ht. 7cm. W. 5.4cm. D. 3.8cm.

An upright rectangular-shaped clock with a black
enamel and gold case set upon a carved black onyx
base. Two cabochon ruby handled doors open to reveal the dial of gold with geometric red and black
enamel designs mounted with rose diamond pointers. The chapter ring includes the inside door
panels and is black enamelled gold with rose diamond Roman numerals.

Fabricator: Coüet Workshop, Paris, for Cartier,
Paris.

Cartier Stock Number: #164322.

Provenance: H. Robert Greene, New York.
Auction: *The H. Robert Greene
Collection of Art Deco*, Christie's,
Geneva, November 16, 1978.
Obsidian, London.
Private Collection, Paris.
Obsidian, London.
The Lindemann Collection, New
York, from 1983.

Comments:

Such pieces were known as "altar" or "shrine"
clocks, the design having been based upon shrines
or altars in western churches and Oriental temples
that open to reveal religious icons or relics.

The Chinese influence upon Cartier's Art Deco
objects was considerable and may be traced to an
origin as early as 1888. However, the first Chinese-
styled pieces (cigarette cases) were not manufac-
tured until 1913. In this dramatic timepiece, Cartier did not rely upon any antique elements,
electing instead to present the clock as a contemporary reinterpretation of Chinese motifs. The
stepped rectangular dial in red and black enamel
and the *pavé*-set diamond Roman numerals against
black enamel, are striking examples of fashionable
Art Deco taste.

The movement of the clock was produced by the
European Watch and Clock Company, a subsidiary
established by Cartier in 1919. "EWC" maintained
branches in both Paris and New York and handled
the export of the Paris clock models.

This clock is accompanied by a fitted red leather
case.

It has been exhibited in: *Cartier, Masterpieces of
20th Century Decorative Art*, Christie's, New York,
April 1985, #46; and *Cartier: The Cartier Room*,
Grosvenor House Antiques Fair, London, 1986,
#121.

Similar clocks are illustrated in: Nadelhoffer,
H., *Cartier: Jewelers Extraordinary*, Thames and
Hudson, 1984, plate 70; *Retrospective Louis Car-
tier, Masterworks of Art Deco*, Los Angeles County
Museum, 1982-1983; and *Retrospective Louis Car-
tier, 101 Years of the Jeweler's Art*, Christie's, New
York, 1976, plate 80.

PLATE LVIII

PAPERWEIGHT CLOCK

Agate, lapis-lazuli, jade, and gold.
1929.

Ht. 1 $^1/_{16}$″ W. 3 $^3/_8$″ D. 4 $^{13}/_{16}$″
Ht. 2.7cm. W. 8.6cm. D. 12.2cm.

A heavy rectangular carved agate case set at the sides with lapis-lazuli mosaics within reeded gold mounts. The clock is set within a gold mount decorated with lapis-lazuli batons and jade cabochons at each corner. The pale green jade dial is mounted with blue enamel and gold Roman numerals and similarly decorated pointers and central motif. In each corner are gold set lapis-lazuli cabochons.

Fabricator: Coüet Workshop, Paris, for Cartier, Paris.

Cartier Stock Number: #2456.

Provenance: Private Collection.
Private Collection.
Obsidian, London.
The Lindemann Collection, New York, from 1987.

Comments:

Paperweight clocks are extremely rare in the *oeuvre* of Cartier; the Lindemann example is the only one known at present. However, the concept of a combined clock and weight appealed to the taste of the 1920s and '30s; this taste favored luxury objects which possessed a pragmatic function. The multipurpose gadget became extremely fashionable around 1930; the era witnessed the production of such objects as letter knives fitted with clocks and magnifying glasses equipped as paper cutters.

Such objects were, however, not inexpensive at the time. The original Cartier worksheet for this paperweight clock reveals that it cost 8890 French francs to fabricate in 1929. It sold for 13,000 French francs, or five hundred and fifty-one 1929 United States dollars. Surprisingly, even at this price, it was sold for much less than the customary one hundred percent mark-up.

This clock is accompanied by its original fitted red leather case.

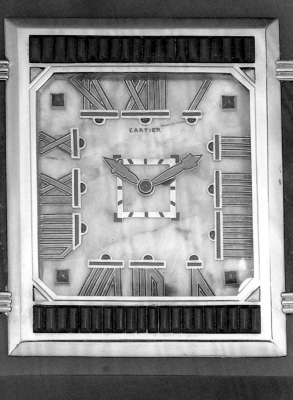

PLATE LIX

"COMET" CLOCK

Rock crystal, diamond, ruby, enamel, and gold.
circa 1921.

Diam. 4"
Diam. 10. 2cm.

The clock is comprised of a rock crystal case bearing two white enamel-on-gold chapter rings. The outer registers minutes and the inner hours; the outer ring is decorated with Arabic numerals interspaced with gold and enamel rosettes. The inner ring is similarly decorated with Roman numerals and is bordered by rose diamonds. The central section of the dial is enamelled in deep 'night sky' blue with gold stars and a long gold and diamond hour hand formed to represent a comet. Around the outer dial a star-shaped ruby and diamond pointer shows the minutes elapsed.

Fabricator: Coüet Workshop, Paris, for Cartier, Paris.

Cartier Stock Number: #415.

Provenance: Mr. Stokes Phelps, 1921.
Cartier, 1923.
Monsieur et Mme. Santu Marissy, 1925.
Obsidian, London.
The Lindemann Collection, New York, from 1984.

Comments:

Predecessor of the famous Mystery clocks, this clock may have been inspired by the work of the seventeenth-century horologist Nicolas Grollier de Servières of Lyons. This example was fabricated by Maurice Coüet (1885-1963), who had produced table clocks for Cartier since 1911. One of Cartier's most talented collaborators, Coüet was fascinated by complex mechanical horological devices and created a series of imaginative clocks firmly based in mathematic principles. The "Comet," or "Planet" clocks were his first invention for Cartier.

They were produced in arched, square, and circular cases.

Hans Nadelhoffer points out that the star decor of the "Comet" clock dials was directly related to the Islamic-styled jewelry that Cartier was simultaneously retailing.

The provenance of this "Comet" clock illustrates an interesting point. At this time, Cartier's frequently repurchased distinguished objects from clients and resold them as stock.

This "Comet" clock is accompanied by the original fitted red leather case.

THE MYSTERY CLOCKS

There is little question that the renowned Mystery clocks of the House of Cartier represent the the zenith of its many achievements. These masterpieces of Art Deco design and technology stand in relation to the House of Cartier as the earlier imperial Russian Easter eggs do to the House of Fabergé. Both are regarded as benchmarks of quality for their respective periods.

The French horological tradition is a distinguished one, and the Cartier firm had early dealt in watches and antique clocks; pocket watches appeared in its inventory as early as 1853. However, it should be stressed that these articles were purchased by the House of Cartier from outside suppliers for resale. Such watches were fabricated of gold, silver, copper, and steel and were frequently embellished according to the dictates of Second Empire (1852-1871) taste with onyx, pearls, and *cloisonné* enamels. In keeping with its early practice of purveying a variety of antique objects, Cartier also sold fine antique watches; early records reveal the sale of an enamelled eighteenth-century watch by Jean-Antoine Lépine (1720-1814), a Louis XIV silver pocket watch, several watches by the Swiss-born French maker Abraham-Louis Breguet (1747-1823) and an early nineteenth-century watch/automaton in the form of a seal fitted with a music box. During 1870s and '80s, gold and enamel chatelaines were popular timepieces retailed by the firm, and these pendant devices included not only watches but fobs, seals, charms, and diminutive coin purses. By the 1890s, Cartier was supplied with fine pocket watches from such prominent makers as Ferdinand Verger of Paris and Vacheron and Constantin of Geneva.

However, when Louis Cartier (1875-1942) joined his father in business in 1898, the time had come for watches and clocks to play a major role in Cartier's history. The move a year later to the rue de la Paix premises only served to strengthen the younger Cartier's contention that table clocks (*pendulettes* and *pendules*) be added to the standard line of pocket watches and chatelaines, that the in-house production of timepieces be built up, and that the firm explore the market potential of the wristwatch.[1]

Louis was allowed to proceed with his ideas, and from 1901 the table clock was a Cartier staple. These clocks were almost always enamelled and exhibited revived Louis XVI motifs. Their chief contribution to the development of the Mystery clocks was in familiarizing Cartier with the mechanics of farming out movement, case, and dial manufacture to several different fabricators. Not suprisingly, the early table clocks relied upon the French-inspired models of the Russian Peter Carl Fabergé.[2]

About this time, *circa* 1909, a young French clockmaker, Maurice Coüet (1885-1963) working in the Prevost *atelier* was developing talents which would eventually cause Cartier's clocks to eclipse all others of the period. The descendant of a line of clock and watch makers, Coüet set up a workshop in the rue Saint-Martin around 1910. He became sufficiently well known within a year to attract the attention of Louis Cartier. By 1911, Coüet was supplying table clocks exclusively to the House of Cartier. This initial collaboration was to evolve into one of the most successful and fruitful of Cartier's associations, for Coüet possessed the same sort of genius that had produced the great French horologists of the Renaissance. He admired complex antique clock mechanisms and particularly enjoyed those which featured illusionistic mechanical devices. Coüet's twentieth-century versions of these past accomplishments were delightfully conceived and took simultaneous advantage of the latest technological innovations. By 1913, the Coüet *atelier* had produced "Comet" or "Planet" clocks (catalogue number LIX); these created the illusion of a time-keeping comet, star, or moon moving across the "sky" of the dial. His 1919 variant of the "Comet" type recalled the imaginative chronoscope creations of the seventeenth-century French master Nicolas Grollier de Servières (1593-1685/86). In the Coüet version, the hour chapter appeared at the left quadrant of the circular frame, whose upper edge was marked with the minutes of the hour, and floated to the sixtieth minute at the far right quadrant where it disappeared, to be replaced by the next hour. In the same year, 1919, Coüet in collaboration with the House of Cartier set up a workshop at 53 rue Lafayette which employed some thirty specialists to produce clocks and movements. Cartier's clocks had by this time become so complex that the staff roster also included enamellers, engine-turners (*guillocheurs*), stone setters, and metalsmiths. Although the entire shop bore the Coüet name, Maurice Coüet worked exclusively on clocks. His workers produced table clocks as well as vanity cases.

The "Comet" or "Planet" clocks originating in 1913 had clearly linked Coüet's name and skills to earlier "mystery" clocks of the seventeenth and nineteenth centuries, the study of which had prepared him for the manufacturing of the great Mystery clocks.[3] Eventually, his Mystery clocks would come to include five distinct types within which categories were complex variations. However, all of these shared the feature of diamond-set hands embedded in a semi-precious dial which kept time with no apparent mechanism. In fact, these dials were formed of sliced faceted polyhedrons of rock crystal, citrine, topaz, or rarely, aquamarine. The pointers were attached to the center slice which in turn was fitted with a toothed metal rim driven by gears disguised within the case of the clock.

The initial Mystery clock of 1913 was entitled "Model A", and it featured a rectangular architectonic case of rock crystal set upon a rectangular hardstone or gold base (catalogue number LX). The second version of 1920 featured a single central axle with a faceted hexagonal hardstone dial set upon a rectangular plinth often fitted with Chinese lambrequin-like feet (catalogue number LXI). The hardstone dial was framed in enamel, lapis-lazuli, coral, or turquoise.

A third type was the *Ecran* (screen) model introduced in 1923; this was the most popular of the three types thus far discussed and was produced with seven variants by 1928. A rare version in moonstone has recently been discovered. The form of the *Ecran* Mystery clock was apparently derived from the traditional French firescreen of the Louis XVI or Empire period and lent itself ideally to the geometrization of the Art Deco taste (catalogue numbers LXII and LXIII).

Also introduced into the Mystery line in 1923 was a fourth type, the so-called "Portico" model (catalogue number LXV). An earlier version of 1920 had appeared in the form of a Chinese gong on stand in which the pendant clock formed the gong. However, this prototype was based upon optical illusion since its mechanism was actually fixed in the base. The six "Portico" Mystery clocks developed between 1923 and 1925 all featured pendant hardstone dials and transmission to the hands via a central axle. Each of the "Portico" models was designed as an Oriental gateway with rock crystal side columns supporting a frieze and cornice surmounted with a Buddha figure or a "Foo" lion.

Glamorous and innovative as these Mystery models were it was the *animalia* or figure subject Mystery clocks which were to receive the greatest international acclaim and establish these creations of the House of Cartier as unsurpassed masterpieces of the twentieth-century jeweler's art. For these, Cartier selected antique Chinese objects of jade, agate, rock crystal, or coral that were incorporated into Mystery clocks either by virtue of the clock's resting on top of the particular object or being placed beside it (catalogue number LXIV). The House of Cartier had already demonstrated its ability to adapt period designs into new and original works of art with such pieces as its pillar clock/barometer after the great French neoclassical designer Jean-Charles Delafosse (1734-1789) and its slightly earlier garland bedecked urn-form table clocks in the Louis XVI taste. However, the *animalia* Mystery clocks took this phenomenon a step further by removing the antique Oriental sculptures from their original context completely and evolving an object totally compatible with the tenets of the reigning Art Deco mode.

Every component of each Mystery clock was produced by hand, and each clock was the result of collaboration among six or seven specialists. The result was that each took from three to twelve months to fabricate, with the elaborate *animalia* versions being the most time consuming. Even with the lengthy time span from time of order to delivery, the Mystery clocks were sufficiently popular between the peak years of production, *circa* 1913 to 1930, for more than ninety to have been produced.[4] Their production was revived after World War II and continued until 1970. Following the 1972 consolidation of the Cartier branches after their initial sale in 1966, the Mystery clocks were again placed in special order production in 1977. Sleek objects in the Art Deco manner had begun to circulate in *avant-garde* circles at that time, and the revived Deco elements of Cartier's Mystery clocks appeared as fresh and inspired as they had in the years of their introduction.

The reputation of the Mystery clocks as Cartier's greatest production is justly deserved. Their design has survived the crucial test of time, and the Lindemann Collection is distinguished by having an example of each major type.[5]

Author's Notes on page 176

PLATE LX

"MODEL A" MYSTERY CLOCK

Rock crystal, onyx, diamond, ruby, and platinum.
circa 1939.

Ht. 5 ½" W. 3 ¾" D. 1 ⅞"
Ht. 14cm. W. 9.5cm. D. 4.8cm.

Designed in the Art Deco style, this clock is a carved cubic rectangular-shaped case set on a black onyx base. The case is mounted with a circular platinum chapter ring, and rose diamond pointers and Roman numerals. The pointers are enhanced with a cabachon ruby collet.

Fabricator: Coüet Workshop, Paris, for Cartier, Paris.

Cartier Stock Number: #39, #01163.

Provenance: Auction: Sotheby's, New York, December 5-6, 1984, #285, illustrated.
The Lindemann Collection, New York, from 1984.

Comments:

The "Model A" was the first of the renowned Cartier Mystery clocks and was designed in 1913; the first "Model A" was sold to J.P. Morgan in that same year. Queen Mary of England acquired an example in 1924, and in 1945, Charles de Gaulle, head of the French Provisional Government, presented one to Joseph Stalin. Although designed during the budding years of the Art Deco style, the "Model A" clock is a classic twentieth-century design, appearing today as contemporary as it did in 1913. Its distinctly architectural character is probably a reflection of Louis Cartier's personal preference for such designs. This taste is also shared by the Lindemanns and marks a number of pieces in their collection.

These mysterious timepieces appear to operate with no connection between the hands and the movement. In fact, the apparently solid rock crystal faces are sliced, the central stratum being a rotating disc containing the hands.

The Mystery clocks, universally accepted as the apogee of Cartier's work during the "Golden Era" years, circa 1919-1939, were result of an extremely successful collaboration between Cartier and Maurice Coüet (1855-1963), whose *atelier* at 53 rue Lafayette, Paris, produced these clocks.

This clock is accompanied by the original Cartier fitted red leather case.

For further comments on Mystery clocks, see catalogue numbers LXI, LXII, LXIII, LXIV, and LXV.

Similar Mystery clocks are illustrated in: Nadelhoffer, H., *Cartier: Jewelers Extraordinary*, Harry N. Abrams, New York, 1984, plate 60; *Retrospective Louis Cartier, Masterworks of Art Deco*, Los Angeles County Museum, 1982-1983, plate 15; and *Retrospective Louis Cartier, 101 Years of the Jeweler's Art*, Cartier, New York, 1976, plate 99.

PLATE LXI

TURQUOISE MYSTERY CLOCK

Rock crystal, turquoise, diamond, wood, enamel, gold, and platinum.
1921.

Ht. 5 ³⁄₈″ W. 3 ¹⁄₄″ D. 1 ⁷⁄₈″
Ht. 13.5cm. W. 8.2cm. D. 4.7cm.

An upright geometric composition mounted on a gold base. The timepiece is a fancy cut hexagonal polyhedron rock crystal dial inlaid with rose diamond pointers, and mounted with a conforming black enamel-on-gold chapter ring. The chapter ring is applied with paired turquoise arabesques enhanced with white and black enamel Roman numerals and a gold bezel. The timepiece is mounted on a black lacquer trapezoidal vasiform pedestal decorated with four gold collet turquoise cabochons atop a rectangular black lacquer plinth. The whole is raised on an Oriental-style gold base with relief geometric banded designs.

Fabricator: Coüet Workshop, Paris, for Cartier, Paris.

Cartier Stock Number: #556.

Provenance: Obsidian, London.
The Lindemann Collection, New York, from 1987.

Comments:

The second model of the famed Mystery clocks, of which this is an example, was introduced in 1920. This particular clock was completed in 1921; however, it was not sold until 1923, an indication of the length of time important pieces frequently remained in the Cartier inventory.

This model of the Mystery clock employed a single central axle passed through the shaft and, later, through a hollow coral sphere. The basic design of the model was altered in nineteen variations until 1931. The variants included an octagonal dial, a circular citrine dial set on an enamelled pillar with lateral struts, and a rectangular cartouche with Japanese corners made of ebonite with a dial formed of a cushion-shaped citrine and a similar rectangular model having bevelled corners. These spectacular examples of the clockmaker's art were the result of a long and fruitful collaboration between the House of Cartier and the talented Maurice Coüet (1885-1963).

The movement of this clock was made by the European Watch and Clock Company, #SS6/4980.

For further comments on the Mystery clocks, see catalogue numbers LX, LXII, LXIII, LXIV, and LXV.

A nearly identical clock is illustrated in: *Retrospective Louis Cartier, 101 Years of the Jeweler's Art,* Cartier, New York, 1976, plate 18.

PLATE LXII

ECRAN MYSTERY CLOCK

Coral, rock crystal, *nacre*, diamond, enamel, and gold.
circa 1928.

Ht. 5 ¼″ W. 4 ¹/₁₆″ D. 2 ¾″
Ht. 12.7cm. W. 10.5cm. D. 7cm.

An upright rectangular-shaped black enamel case on a black enamel and gold base. The case is mounted with a dodecagonal rock crystal dial set with rose diamond pointers. The dial is surrounded with a *nacre* chapter ring with black enamel borders and Roman numerals, and a rose diamond inner bezel. Rose diamond set spandrels complete the central motif. The case is further enhanced with bands of baton coral in gold channel settings repeated along the sides and above and below the dial. It is supported on the base by two carved rock crystal arches and a central carved coral bead.

Fabricator: Coüet Workshop, Paris, for Cartier, Paris.

Cartier Stock Number: #1675.

Provenance: King Farouk of Egypt.
Auction: Sotheby's, St. Moritz, February 21-23, 1985, #770, color illustration, Plate CXI.
The Lindemann Collection, New York, from 1985.

Comments:

The rectangular *Ecran* Mystery clock appeared in 1923; seven variants of it had been produced by 1928. Although Hans Nadelhoffer stated in *Cartier: Jewelers Extraordinary* (Harry N. Abrams, New York, 1984) that the *Ecran* clock was sufficiently popular to remain in production until 1954, it is now widely believed that only eight *Ecran* models exist. Five of these carry the horizontal coral batons observed here, while two bear jade decorations, and a recently discovered model is decorated in

moonstone. All the models share the characteristic vertical form which appears to have been inspired by a late eighteenth or early nineteenth-century firescreen, whose outline is still detectable in this highly geometric Art Deco object.

The celebrated Mystery clocks of the House of Cartier were the result of an inspired longterm collaboration between Louis Cartier and Maurice Coüet (1885-1963). Coüet was descended from a line of clock and watch makers and was fascinated by elaborate illusionistic clock movements. This suited him ideally to the concepts of clock design which Cartier was formulating. The *Ecran* Mystery clock was the third model produced in the series. The first was the "Model A" (catalogue number LX) created in 1913, and the second model equipped with a single axle and an octagonal or circular dial and case set upon a rectangular base (catalogue number LXI) was formulated in 1920.

The movement of this clock was made by the European Watch and Clock Company.

King Farouk frequently patronized the firm of Cartier and acquired a wide variety of objects from it, including a number of clocks. This Mystery clock was perhaps his most important purchase at Cartier's. Originally, the plinth of the clock bore the applied crowned cipher of Farouk in diamonds; when the clock was confiscated by the Egyptian government, the cipher was removed. When acquired by the Lindemanns a script "L" was designed to fit the piercings indicating the location of the original monogram.

For further comments on the Mystery clocks, see catalogue numbers LX, LXI, LXIII, LXIV, and LXV.

Similar clocks are illustrated in: *Retrospective Louis Cartier, Masterworks of Art Deco*, Los Angeles County Museum, 1982-1983, plates 52 and 101; and *Retrospective Louis Cartier, 101 Years of the Jeweler's Art*, Cartier, New York, 1976, plate 105.

PLATE LXIII

ECRAN MYSTERY CLOCK/ STANDISH

Grey and white agate, rock crystal, diamond,
enamel, and gold.
1925.

Ht. 7″ W. 11″ D. 5 ¾″
Ht. 18cm. W. 28cm. D. 14.5cm.

A rectangular-shaped case atop a carved grey agate
base. The centrally positioned case is coral-colored
and black enamel with apertures at the top displaying the day, date, and month. It is mounted
with a circular rock crystal dial and spandrels. The
dial is embedded with foliage-shaped rose diamond
pointers carrying black enamel borders and is surrounded with a white enamel chapter ring decorated with gold Roman numerals and a rose
diamond inner bezel. The center of the base is fitted with a concave carved pen tray equipped with
a gold pencil. The tray and timepiece are flanked
by a pair of vasiform Chinese-style white agate ink-
stands; each of the oval lobed bodies is lined in
gold, supported on four openwork feet, and has
carved floral handles and a lotus finial cover. The
covers are further enhanced with two gold lined
rings.

Fabricator: Designed by Alexandre Diringer,
Coüet Workshop, Paris, for Cartier, Paris.

Cartier Stock Number: #332.

Provenance: Auction: Christie's, Geneva, May 16,
1985, #332, illustrated.
The Lindemann Collection, New
York, from 1985.

Comments:

This is the only known Mystery clock which Cartier incorporated into an elaborate jeweled desk set,
and was originally commissioned by one of Cartier's
princely Indian clients.

The model of the clock is that of the *écran*, or
screen, the form of which was apparently inspired
by a Louis XVI or Empire fireplace screen. The
streamlined outline clearly recalls that of its im-

portant eighteenth-century prototype. The first
Ecran clock was produced by the House of Cartier
in 1923.

Louis Cartier was justifiably proud and secretive
of the Mystery clocks and attempted to keep the
method of their fabrication concealed. Cartier's
great collaborator on these clocks was the talented
Maurice Coüet (1885-1963), who had begun his
career at the Prevost workshop and was later to
raise Cartier's table and mantel clocks to the level
of masterpieces.

The incorporation of the uniquely Cartier *Ecran*
clock into this massive standish reflects the fascination of the Art Deco period with objects which
served many purposes within a single framework.
The combination of the *Ecran* clock case with the
Chinese-style inkwells is indicative of Cartier's
brilliant eclecticism by which a wide variety of design elements were integrated into a single bold
statement at once decorative and functional.

This clock is accompanied by its original fitted
red leather case.

For further comments on the Mystery clocks, see
catalogue numbers LX, LXI, LXII, LXIV, and
LXV.

PLATE LXIV

"MANDARIN DUCK" MYSTERY CLOCK

Topaz, jade, ruby, onyx, diamond, enamel, gold, and platinum.
1922, the duck *circa* 1800.

Ht. 10½" W. 6" D. 4"
Ht. 26.7cm. W. 15.3cm. D. 10.2cm.

A carved duck of pale green Chinese jade from the Ch'ing Dynasty (1644-1911) studded with gold collet cabochon rubies. The bird sets on a carved black onyx plinth atop an Oriental-style gold base. The center back of the duck is mounted with dodecagonal polyhedron topaz dial secured by a black enamel on gold caparison. The clock pointers are *pavé*-set diamonds as is the bezel. The dial is surrounded by a similarly shaped chapter ring in blue enamel with white enamel Roman numerals.

Fabricator: Coüet Workshop, Paris, for Cartier, Paris.

Cartier Stock Number: #0139.

Provenance: Sir B. Abdy.
Cartier, New York.
The Lindemann Collection, New York, from 1983.

Comments:

At approximately the same time that the three regular Mystery clock models ("Model A," catalogue number LXIII; Model 2, catalogue number LXIV; and the *Ecran* clocks, catalogue numbers LXV and LXVI), Cartier and Coüet created a series of twelve *animalia* or figure clocks whose principal feature was a dial supported from below, as here, or suspended from above. The form of these clocks was derived from Louis XV and Louis XVI *pendules à sujet* in which the clock movement and dial rested on the back of an animal such as a rhinoceros, elephant, horse, or bull. These eighteenth-century prototypes had generally been executed in patinated or gilt bronze. The scale of the "Mandarin Duck" Mystery clock is also that of its eighteenth-century prototype. Like other celebrated French designers of the Art Deco period, Louis Cartier held objects of the eighteenth century in considerable respect.

The "Mandarin Duck" Mystery clock of 1922 was the first of this series. Regarded in their time as the most prestigious of Cartier productions, the clocks of this series are today the most esteemed—and valuable—of all collector's items bearing the Cartier signature.

For all of the Mystery clocks, Cartier employed a faceted rock crystal, topaz, citrine, or, rarely, aquamarine dial. The transparency of these materials in no way detracted from the apparently embedded pointers which had no visible works.

The "Mandarin Duck" Mystery clock is not only a masterpiece of the horologist's art; it also demonstrates the genius of Louis Cartier and his designers for reworking a period object into a new, entirely viable, context. Here the Ch'ing Dynasty jade duck, *circa* 1800, has become a modish Art Deco object. This miraculous transformation has been effected without straining the design concept.

Although Cartier apparently selected antique Chinese hardstone objects for incorporation into the *animalia* series, it is possible that the "Mandarin Duck" base of this clock was chosen for its specific significance. In traditional Chinese iconography, the duck is a symbol of conjugal fidelity since it mates for life. It is, therefore, a fitting motif for a object intended as a wedding or anniversary presentation.

Although the "Mandarin Duck" Mystery clock has traditionally been catalogued as having a dial of faceted citrine, the original Cartier work sheet for the clock, now in the possession of the Musée Cartier, Geneva, Switzerland, lists this as being *"une grosse topaze"* (an enormous topaz). Accordingly, the corrected term topaz has been used in this publication.

This clock is illustrated in: Nadelhoffer, H., *Cartier: Jewelers Extraordinary*, Harry N. Abrams, New York, 1984, plate 68; and *Retrospective Louis Cartier, Masterworks of Art Deco*, Los Angeles County Museum, 1982-1983, plate 95.

For further comments on the Mystery clocks, see catalogue numbers LX, LXI, LXII, LXIII, and LXV.

PLATE LXV

"PORTICO" MYSTERY CLOCK

Rock crystal, onyx, agate, diamond, coral,
enamel, and gold.
1924.

Ht. 13³/₄″ W. 9¹/₄″ D. 4³/₄″
Ht. 35cm. W. 23.5cm. D. 12cm.

An upright open case atop a polished gold base.
The case consists of two rock crystal columns bearing black enamel on gold ornamentation enhanced
with gold rondelles and platforms. The columns are
set on square agate plinths faced with stepped rock
crystal braces. A black onyx entabulature bridges
the columns and is decorated with cabochon rubies
and a central carved rock crystal Buddha. A dodecagonal polyhedron rock crystal dial is centrally
suspended from the lintel by a gold bow and an Oriental-style bracket. A rock crystal stretcher pierces
the column capitals. The dial is set with rose diamond pointers and surrounded by black enamel
chapter ring secured by a gold bezel. The rose diamond Roman numerals are interspaced with lambrequin motifs and stripes in gold.

Fabricator: Coüet Workshop, Paris, for Cartier,
    Paris.

Cartier Stock Number: #6744.

Provenance: Auction: Christie's, Geneva,
    November 14, 1985, #417,
    illustrated.
    The Lindemann Collection, New
    York, from 1985.

Comments:

This "Portico," or "Temple Gate" clock is one of
six made by Cartier between 1923 and 1925. They
represent the quintessential solution to the problems which Mystery clocks posed.

The Cartier Mystery clocks (*pendules mystérieuses*) are today regarded as the zenith of the many
achievements of the House of Cartier. They are Cartier's undisputed masterpieces and are to the
House of Cartier what the imperial Russian Easter
eggs were to the House of Fabergé.

The development of these celebrated clocks was
the result of an inspired collaboration between
Louis Cartier and Maurice Coüet (1885-1963)
which began in 1911. Coüet descended from a line
of clock and watchmakers and was fascinated by
mysterious mechanical illusions. He probably knew
something of the seventeenth-century *horloges mystérieuses* created by Nicolas Grollier de Servières of
Lyons (1593-1685/86). These may have served as
the inspiration for the Mystery clocks created for
the House of Cartier at Coüet's workshop at 53 rue
Lafayette, Paris.

The dials of the Mystery clocks, as here, were
generally of rock crystal. Its innate transparency
did not detract from the illusion of the hands being
trapped inside. Occasionally, citrine, topaz, or
rarely, aquamarine was also used (i.e. the "Mandarin Duck" Mystery clock, catalogue number
LXIV).

The markedly architectural format of the aptly
named "Portico" clock had its design origins in the
mantel clocks of the Louis XVI period. The airy
neoclassical compositions of that era eventually became a standard decorating accessory during the
Restauration (1814-1824) and Charles X (1824-
1830) periods. These later neoclassical mantel
clocks were distinctly architectonic in character
and featured prominent friezes and cornices supported by sturdy columns between which were
placed the dial and pendulum.

This clock is accompanied by a fitted red leather
case.

It is illustrated in: Nadelhoffer, H., *Cartier: Jewelers Extraordinary*, Harry N. Abrams, New York,
1984, plate 54.

For further comments on the Mystery clocks, see
catalogue numbers LX, LXI, LXII, LXIII, and
LXIV.

Similar clocks are illustrated in: *Retrospective
Louis Cartier, Masterworks of Art Deco*, Los Angeles
County Museum, 1982-1983, plate 4; and *Retrospective Louis Cartier, 101 Years of the Jeweler's Art*,
Cartier, New York, 1976, plate 100.

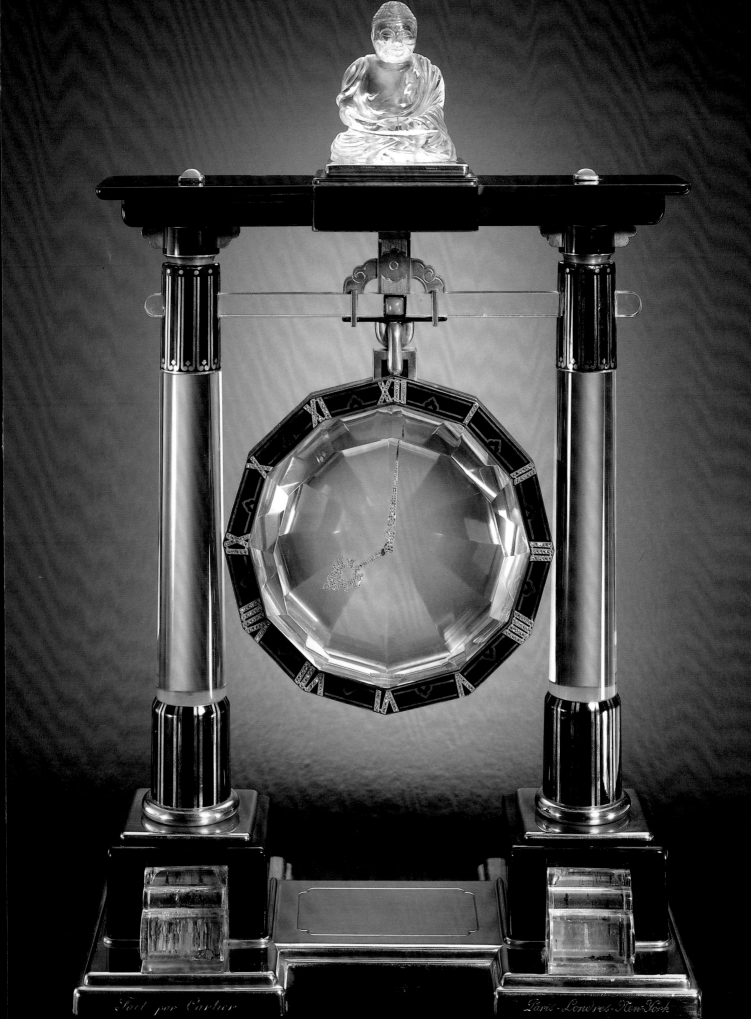

Continued from page 150

Continued from page 163

POCKET WATCH

Onyx, diamond, enamel, gold, and platinum.
circa 1930-1932.

Ht. 2 ¼″ Diam. 1 ¾″, Ht. 5.8cm. Diam. 4.5cm.

A circular carved black onyx case with a platinum
geometric bow, capstan and *pavé*-set diamond decorative rim. The case is mounted with a white on
white enamel dial, blue enamel Breguet pointers
and black enamel chapter ring with applied rose
diamond Roman numerals. The rock crystal glass
is held by a delicate gold bezel.

Fabricator: Cartier, New York.

Cartier Stock Number: number inside case.

Provenance: Joseph S. Lindemann, New York.
The Lindemann Collection, New
York, from 1985.

Comments:

The starkly dramatic contrasts of black onyx,
white enamel, and diamonds admirably suited the
elegant aesthetic of the 1930s. Although by this
time, Cartier's exclusive clientele had successfully
been persuaded that the modernity of the wristwatch was acceptable, pocket watches continued to
be the correct accessorizing timepiece for men's
formal wear. The tailored opulence of this example
would have made it the ideal companion for traditional white tie or dinner attire. Such classic con-
fections today bear mute witness to the
inventiveness and taste of the House of Cartier during the "Golden Era" years, *circa* 1919-1939.

Similar pocket watches are illustrated in: *Retrospective Louis Cartier, Masterworks of Art Deco*,
Los Angeles County Museum, 1982-1983, plate
82; and *Retrospective Louis Cartier, 101 Years of the
Jeweler's Art*, Cartier, New York, 1976, plate 64.

[1] *Louis Cartier felt adamantly that the wristwatch was the form
of the future. Subsequent developments were to prove him correct although contemporary fashion critics and watch buyers ridiculed the
new watch form as effete, effeminate, and excessively radical.*

[2] *Cartier ordered some of its table clock cases from such Russian suppliers as the Moscow firm of Yahr.* Nadelhoffer, H. *Cartier:
Jewelers Extraordinary*, Harry N. Abrams, New York, 1984, p. 246.

[3] For a full discussion of this evolution, see Nadelhoffer, H.,
Cartier: Jewelers Extraordinary, Harry N. Abrams, New York, 1984,
pp. 245-254.

[4] Nadelhoffer, H., *Cartier: Jewelers Extraordinary*, Harry N.
Abrams, New York, 1984, p. 251.

[5] In the instance of the *Ecran* clock (catalogue numbers LXII)
the Lindemann Collection includes both the standard mantel/desk
model and a unique version incorporating the *Ecran* form into a massive Art Deco standish (catalogue number LXIII).

GLOSSARY

annulus. In the form of an unbroken ring or circle.

atelier. A workshop or studio and, collectively, group of workmen or artisans.

baguette. A gemstone cut in a flat rectangular shape bordered with four step-cut facets.

baton. A gemstone cut similar to the baguette, but longer and not necessarily faceted.

bezel. The metal rim on the front of a watch or clock case in which the crystal is set. The metal rim on a finger ring which holds the stone or ornament. The rim or band surrounding the top of a box on which the lid rests. Also, the former name describing the facets of the crown of a brilliant cut gemstone.

black onyx. Chalcedony dyed black.

bowenite. A variety of hard serpentine ranging in color from pale grey to cream.

brilliant. A gem cut which is usually rounded or oval and includes many facets to minimize the amount of light escaping from the bottom of the gemstone.

cabochon. A stone cut with a smooth rounded highly polished surface without facets.

calibré. A gem cut which is often oblong or eliptical so that it can be placed side-by-side with similarly cut other stones in snugly fitting groups.

case. The structure which encloses the watch or clock workings.

channel setting. A style of securing rows of identically shaped square or rectangular gemstones between two adjoined bands.

chinoiserie. European decoration inspired by fanciful Oriental sources, particularly Chinese, but often incorporating Japanese and Islamic motifs.

claw-setting. A style of securing a gem by using a series of projecting prongs which are crimped over the edges of the stone.

collet. A circular metal band in which gems can be held.

cushion-shaped. A gem cut which produces a rounded square or rectangular-shaped stone.

double clip. A type of clip which can be divided and worn as separate components or integrated to form a single brooch.

ebonite. A hard vulcanized rubber: used by Cartier on the second model of the Mystery clocks on the corners.

égyptérie. European decoration inspired from ancient Egyptian sources, often incorporating parts of genuine artifacts, and employing shapes, color combinations, textures and patterns associated with Pharoanic Egypt.

Egyptian faïence. A ware made in Egypt before 3000 BC which is composed of fused ground quartz covered with a pulverized and emulsified colored quartz glazing to produce a decorative medium which ranges in color from green to dark blue.

guilloché **enamel.** a method of decoration in which a glaze of transparent enamel is applied over engine-turned metal producing a solid colored, but patterned surface.

jasper. An opaque variety of quartz.

joaillerie. A French term which refers to jewelry in general also, a type of jewelry composed mainly of gemstones.

keystone. Gem cut which produces a stone with an isosceles trapezoid table bordered with trapezoid facets.

lapis-lazuli. A deep-blue colored complex stone composed of hauyne, lazuite, sodalite, and calcite, often containing pyrite inclusions.

lacque burgauté. A rare 18th century Chinese lacquered mother-of-pearl, often enhanced with dyes to accentuate the pinks, blues, and other colors inherent in the material. Nadelhoffer cautions the use of this term in reference to the work of Cartier, because in 1862, it originally described porcelain with mother-of-pearl lacquer.

lunette. A watch or clock crystal which is convex-shaped.

marquise. A modified brilliant cut which produces an elliptical stone pointed on both ends, also referred to as a navette.

Moghul. Indian jewelry made during the Moghul Empire from about 1526 to 1707 and for some time during the period of British control.

moonstone. A transparent or translucent variety of feldspar which ranges in color from a bluish sheen to white.

mother-of-pearl. The hard, smooth iridescent inner lining of the shell of certain mollusks consisting mainly of layers of calcium carbonate and conchiolin which create the opalescent surface, also called *nacre.*

mount. The framework in which gemstones are set.

nacre. see mother-of-pearl.

nephrite. One of two gemstones commonly referred to as jade; it is less hard than jadeite, the other variety, and ranges in color from white to dark green and shades of grey or brown to black.

onyx. A black and white layered variety of chalcedony.

"panther" pattern. A term referring to a frequently used Cartier motif composed of *pavé*-set diamonds interspersed with fancy cut onyx cabochons.

pavé-**setting.** A style of securing many small gemstones very close together in a mass so as to cover the surface and conceal the metal base.

pendules à sujet. A style of Louis XV and Louis XVI clock composed of a movement supported on the back of an animal or figure.

rose diamond. A term used interchangeably to describe a diamond formed in one of the many symmetrical rose-cut styles or one of such small size that it can be cut only a small amount or not at all.

seed pearl. A small pearl weighing less than one-quarter of a grain.

style guirlande. A style of French jewelry which was a revival of the King Louis XV and Louis XVI styles characterized for its symmetrical shapes and decoration of garlands, wreaths, bowknots and tassels.

table. The flat surface which is the top of a cut gemstome.

trillion. A cutting of a gemstone which produces a triangular shaped table bordered by isosceles trapeziod facets.

ziggurat. Any one of the distinctive stepped pyramids found in Mesopotamia in the fertile crescent between the Tigres and Euphrates rivers.

SELECTED BIBLIOGRAPHY

Books

Black, J.A., *A History of Jewelry*, New York, 1981.

Culme, J. and N. Rayner, *The Jewels of the Duchess of Windsor*, London and New York, 1987.

Garside, A., ed., *Jewelry, Ancient to Modern*, New York, 1979.

Gautier, G., *Cartier: The Legend*, Arlington Books, London, 1983.

Hinks, P., *Nineteenth Century Jewellery*, London, 1955.

Lothringen, G. von Habsburg and A. von Solodkoff, *Fabergé, Court Jeweler to the Tsars*, New York, 1979.

Nadelhoffer, H., *Cartier: Jewelers Extraordinary*, New York, 1984.

Newman, H., *An Illustrated Dictionary of Jewelry*, London, 1981.

Sataloff, J. and A. Richards, *The Pleasure of Jewelry and Gemstones* , London, 1975.

Snowman, K. A., *Carl Fabergé, Goldsmith to the Imperial Court of Russia*, New York, 1979

Snowman, K. A., *The Art of Carl Fabergé*, London, 1955.

Tait, H., *Jewellery through 7000 Years*, London, 1976.

Tait, H. and C. Gere, *The Jeweller's Art, An Introduction to the Hull Gundy Gift to the British Museum*, London, 1978.

Vever, H., *La Bijouterie française du XIXème siècle*, Paris, 1906.

Exhibition Catalogues

A La Vieille Russie, *Fabergé, a Loan Exhibition for the Benefit of the Cooper-Hewitt Museum*, New York, April 22-May 21, 1983.

Cartier, *The Cartier Museum at the Goldsmith's Hall*, Foster Lane, London, 23 May-10 June 1988.

Cartier, *Retrospective Louis Cartier, Masterworks of Art Deco*, Los Angeles County Museum, 1982-1983.

Cartier, *Retrospective Louis Cartier, 101 Years of the Jeweler's Art*, New York, October 13-October 29, 1976.

Lothringen, G. von Habsburg, *Fabergé, Hofjuwelier der Zaren*, Kunsthalle der Hypo-Kulturstiftung, Munich, Germany, December 5, 1986-22 February, 1987.

Victoria and Albert Museum, *Fabergé: 1846-1920*, June 23-September 25, 1977.

Walters Art Gallery, Baltimore, Maryland, and the American Federation of Arts, New York, *Objects of Adornment, Five Thousand Years of Jewelry from the Walters Art Gallery*, Baltimore, 1984, travelling exhibition, October 1984-February 1987.

Sales Catalogues

Christies' International, S.A., *The H. Robert Greene Collection of Art Deco*, Geneva, November 16, 1978.

Sotheby's Inc., *The Jewels of the Duchess of Windsor*, Geneva, April 2-3, 1987.

INDEX